EXPLORATIONS
IN CONVENTION
DECISION MAKING

EXPLORATIONS IN CONVENTION DECISION MAKING

The Democratic Party in the 1970s

Denis G. Sullivan
DARTMOUTH COLLEGE

Jeffrey L. Pressman
MASSACHUSETTS INSTITUTE OF TECHNOLOGY

F. Christopher Arterton
YALE UNIVERSITY

W. H. Freeman and Company
San Francisco

62189

Library of Congress Cataloging in Publication Data

Sullivan, Denis G.
    Explorations in convention decision making.

    Includes index.
    1. Democratic Party.   National Convention,
Miami Beach, Fla., 1972.
    2. Democratic Party.   I.   Pressman, Jeffrey L.,
joint author.   II.   Arterton, F. Christopher, joint
author.   III.   Title.
JK2313 1972.S84   329'.0221'0973   76-4527
ISBN 0-7167-0488-9
ISBN 0-7167-0487-0 pbk.

Printed in the United States of America

9 8 7 6 5 4 3 2 1

To our parents

Contents

62189

Preface

This book is a continuation of our theoretical and empirical study of those peculiar organizational forms called presidential nominating conventions. The theoretical questions we explore here first received sustained attention in Denis G. Sullivan, Jeffrey L. Pressman, Benjamin I. Page, and John J. Lyons, *The Politics of Representation: The Democratic Convention 1972* (New York: St. Martin's Press, 1974). In that book we examined the impact of the McGovern-Fraser Commission reforms on the convention process of the Democratic Party. One of the reforms proposed in 1972 was that the Democratic Party adopt a charter (or constitution) and hold midterm policy conferences. The party agreed in Miami to reassemble at a midterm conference in December 1974 at Kansas City to consider the adoption of a charter prepared by Terry Sanford's Charter Commission.

Since the charter proposals and the politics of their adoption touched so many of the theoretical issues we had looked at in 1972, we thought it might be useful to reassemble much of the research team that had worked at Miami and travel to Kansas City in 1974.

The interviewing team of undergraduate and graduate students had proved so successful at Miami that we decided to recruit our new team in the same way. Undergraduate interviewers were selected from Dartmouth College, M.I.T., Wellesley College, and Smith College; a few graduate student interviewers were included from M.I.T. Finally, two faculty members from Dartmouth College also participated as interviewers. On December 5, 1974, the fifteen-member research group boarded a charter flight in Boston bound for Kansas City, Missouri.

The sample of convention delegates was prepared by Robert Saltzman and K. Reimann of Dartmouth College from a list graciously supplied by staff members of the Democratic National Committee: Mark Siegel, Dorothy Bush, and Sheilah Hixson. We should also like to thank Penn Kemble of the Coalition for a Democratic Majority, as well as Alan Baron and Amy Isaacs of the Democratic Planning Group, for their help in preparing the sample.

To our interviewers at Kansas City—Jonathan Fine, Gregory Payne, K. Reimann, Robert Saltzman, Professor Robert T. Nakamura, and Professor Richard F. Winters of Dartmouth College; Daniel Gantt, Robert Johnson, and Neil Weiner of M.I.T.; Madonna Malin of Wellesley College; Andrea Wolfman of Smith College; and Janet Arterton—we express our appreciation for a difficult job well done.

The data from questionnaires and interviews were prepared for statistical analysis by Robert Saltzman, Robert Tarr, and Michael Sandoe with care and persistence. The reliability of their work was gratifyingly high. We owe thanks to David Lucchini and Bruce Backa of Dartmouth College's Project IMPRESS for adapting the data for computer statistical analysis, which was greatly facilitated by Project IMPRESS; and to our typist, Donna Musgrove, whose work was impeccable.

As in 1972, we are indebted to the Ford Foundation for a grant that made this research possible. William Grinker, at that time a Ford Foundation project officer, deserves our special thanks for his help in 1972 and 1974.

We should like to thank our colleagues for their comments on the earlier versions of the manuscript: Benjamin I. Page of The University of Chicago; Judson L. James of Virginia Polytechnic

Institute; Robert T. Nakamura, Richard F. Winters, and Larry Radway of Dartmouth College.

The authors are happy to take full responsibility for this book; the Ford Foundation, Dartmouth College, M.I.T., and Yale University share none of it. Yet each of the authors is more responsible for certain chapters than for others. Chapter 1, dealing with the history of nominating conventions, was written by Jeffrey L. Pressman and F. Christopher Arterton. Chapter 4, on the institutionalization of the caucus movement, and Chapter 7, on party reform, were written by Pressman. Denis G. Sullivan and F. Christopher Arterton wrote Chapter 3, on reform issues and party cleavages. Sullivan wrote Chapter 2, on changes in the political environment of nominating conventions, Chapter 5, on the process of legitimation, and Chapter 6, on theories of convention decision making.

February 1976

Denis G. Sullivan
Dartmouth College

Jeffrey L. Pressman
M.I.T.

F. Christopher Arterton
Yale University

Introduction: Party Conventions in a Time of Social Change

Since their emergence in the first half of the nineteenth century, national party conventions have been a significant feature of the American political landscape, performing important functions for parties and for the broader political system. Observers have frequently pointed out that nominating conventions are often more important than the general elections that follow them, but there has been little systematic work on how decisions are made, legitimated, or perceived by the delegates to those conventions. This gap in the literature seems particularly unfortunate at a time when there is much public debate about the efficacy and equity of the nominating process itself.

Our study focuses on convention behavior, rules changes, and underlying problems of the contemporary Democratic Party in an attempt to understand better what actually goes on at party conventions and conferences. But before examining and discussing convention behavior, we must first consider why the study of party conventions is important.

Party Conventions and the Political System

The first reason for studying conventions is that they play an important role in the American political system. In selecting candidates for President and Vice President, nominating conventions determine the choice that the public will have in the November general elections. Such conventions also ratify a party platform, which sets out the party's position on a wide range of public issues. Furthermore, the national convention is the supreme decision-making body for the party. Thus, conventions may vote on rules for delegate selection, on the composition of the national committee, or on the procedures to be used in the credentials committee, among other items. At the 1968 Democratic convention, for example, delegates voted to form two commissions to reassess and change a number of delegate-selection and convention practices, and required that these commissions deliver reports to the 1972 convention. And in 1974, the Democrats held an unusual mid-term convention for the express purpose of approving a party charter.

Beyond the formal business of conventions, these party meetings serve a number of informal functions. They are occasions for party members to come together to discuss common problems. And they also function as an arena in which bargaining may take place between the various interests, geographical sections, and ideological persuasions within the party. Conventions provide an opportunity for party leaders to find out about the concerns of rank-and-file members, and to receive signals of change or disenchantment at the grass roots. Finally, the opportunity to attend a convention is a reward for party service and can be an incentive for men and women to volunteer their time for party work.

Conventions also provide the social scientist with rich material for analysis; patterns of behavior observed at party conventions can shed light on a number of larger analytical issues.

Because conventions bring together a large number of political leaders, they offer a chance to study both the attitudes of political elites and the ways in which these people interact with each other. Political parties are not monolithic in their views or demographic characteristics, and the study of conventions can reveal the evolving structure of cleavages within the parties. Particularly in a time of party polarization, the depth and persistence of cleavages are matters of concern to party leaders. Do party divisions diminish as various factions interact with each other, or does intraparty bitterness increase? And how do different attitudes toward policy relate to differences over party-reform questions?

Furthermore, examining the behavior of delegates over a period of time can add to our knowledge of political style. How do political activists see their role in the system? What are their goals? Why are they involved in party activity? Are they rigid ideologues, or are they willing to compromise? These questions of political style have been of continuing interest to social scientists, and their significance extends well beyond the conventions themselves.

The study of conventions is also a source of insight into the processes of collective decision making among large groups of people. Given a short period of time, a large degree of uncertainty, and a generally hectic atmosphere, how do people come together to make decisions? Which groups—state delegations, candidate organizations, special group caucuses, and so forth—are most important in the bargaining that takes place? How do these groups organize themselves at the convention? And what strategies do they use in trying to achieve their goals?

After the smoke has cleared and the decisions have been made, the party must find ways to bind up its wounds, to ensure that those who have lost will be able to live with the result. If the various segments of the party believe that the procedures and decisions were fair and proper, and that the final result should be supported, then we may say that "legitimation" has taken place. But legitimation is by no means automatic, as the divisive Republican convention of 1964 and the Democratic conventions of 1968 and 1972 have clearly shown. Thus we are brought to another continuing concern of social scientists: Under what conditions does legitimation take place? How can an organization made of diverse groups integrate its various parts to achieve a common purpose? By studying the ways in which convention groups react to victory, defeat, and each other, we can shed some light on this set of problems.

There has been much talk during recent years about reform of the nominating process. Some proponents of change have called for revisions of the rules for selecting delegates and conducting conventions, while others have suggested the abolition of conventions and their replacement by a single national primary. We believe that consideration of such changes should be informed by careful observation and analysis of how conventions actually work, and we shall return to the issue of reform at the end of this book.

Early Historical Developments

We have sketched out the significance of party conventions for the political system and for the analysis of political behavior. Now we can briefly review the early development of such conventions in the United States, and then turn our attention to some recent changes in the convention process.

The first presidential nominations were not made by conventions, but by the congressional caucus of each party.[1] However, after the Federalist Party's representation in Congress was sharply reduced by electoral defeat in 1800, the caucus could not claim to speak for the party as a whole. The Federalists had to devise other means for selecting a candidate. In 1808, at a secret meeting of party leaders in New York, Thomas Pinckney was nominated for President and Rufus King was nominated for Vice President. According to historian S. E. Morison, "This was the original national nominating convention."[2]

Congressional caucuses as nominating bodies were further weakened by the successive presidential campaigns of Andrew Jackson. As a candidate in 1824, Jackson had little support in Congress; therefore, his supporters attempted to discredit the caucus itself as an institution. They refused to have anything to do with the 1824 Republican caucus, and Jackson ultimately received more electoral votes than William H. Crawford, the caucus nominee. In 1828, state conventions, state legislatures, and state legislative caucuses met to nominate Andrew Jackson.

In 1831 the Anti-Masonic Party held what is often regarded as the first national convention. In that same year, a national Democratic convention met to ratify Jackson's choice of Martin Van Buren as his running mate. Still another national party meeting was held in 1831, as the National Republican convention endorsed a foregone conclusion by nominating Henry Clay for President. Thus, national conventions met initially to ratify decisions previously agreed upon, rather than to forge unity among diverse party factions.

But in 1839, the Whig Party did hold a convention without prior agreement upon a nominee, and the result contributed to party cohesion. Their meeting, held at Harrisburg, Pennsylvania, resulted in the agreement to unite around a national hero, "Old Tippecanoe" William Henry Harrison.[3] The Democratic convention of 1844 saw the creation of a consensus around James K. Polk, whose nomination was certainly not a foregone conclusion; indeed, he had no support on the first ballot.

Since American parties are broad, diverse coalitions of interests, there has always existed the critical problem of procedures through which the various segments of the party could be brought to support the candidacy of someone other than their first choice. The meetings in 1839 and 1844, which facilitated the building of party unity behind a nominee, were early examples of legitimating conventions. As political events, they mark an important step in the institutionalization of procedures to surmount this difficult political problem.[4] Reviewing this early historical experience, V. O. Key concluded,

> Thus there developed a mechanism through which party leaders, dispersed over a nation of continental proportions, could negotiate sufficient agreement to maintain parties capable of governing through the presidential system.[5]

In assessing the performance of the nomination process, political scientists have generally ranked conventions high as arenas for integrating interests and selecting candidates.[6] According to the classic model of convention decision making, important party leaders bargain with each other and make compromises in the interests of victory in November. Thus, we should remember that the goal of a convention is not simply to choose an acceptable nominee, but to choose one who can win the general election. Legitimation has been assumed to be a necessary ingredient to attain that end.

Events of recent years, however, have shaken the faith of many observers in the ability of conventions to knit together the diverse factions of a party. At the same time, changes in convention procedures have taken place that require modification of the traditional view of national conventions as dominated by a small group of high party officials.

Demands for Change and the System's Response: 1968 and After

Although both parties have altered their convention rules since the late 1960s, the strongest demands for change, the most pronounced alterations in the nomination system, and the greatest degree of internal turbulence have been in the Democratic Party. Thus, this book will focus on the Democrats.

Much of the impetus for Democratic convention reform grew out of the 1968 nomination campaign and the turbulent national convention in Chicago. In the aftermath of that convention, Senator George McGovern—who had unsuccessfully sought the presidential nomination—wrote,

> The Democratic National Convention of 1968 already has settled into the folklore of American politics. Its mere mention evokes the vision of tumultuous floor debate, bloodshed and tear gas in the streets, demonstrators and delegates standing together, arm-in-arm, in confrontation with the police. To some it also evokes the image of rigged procedures, of a political past assembled to reach predetermined decisions. The convention became the shame of the Democratic Party and in all likelihood assured its defeat in the November follow up. Wherever politicians meet—wherever Americans meet—they agree that the convention imposed such a strain on the democratic system of government that a repetition would be intolerable.[7]

Although McGovern, as a member of a losing faction, exaggerated the rigged nature of the 1968 convention, his criticisms of that convention were shared by many liberal Democrats who opposed the Vietnam War. In that convention, supporters of anti-war candidates (Senator McGovern, Senator Eugene McCarthy, and the late Senator Robert F. Kennedy) lost out to supporters of Vice President Hubert Humphrey, the candidate of the "regular" Democrats. Members of the losing side complained that their anti-war views were effectively shut out of the convention, and some delegates joined the anti-war demonstrations in the streets outside the convention hall. Going beyond the issue of the Vietnam War, the McCarthy-Kennedy-McGovern supporters argued that the entire nominating system was closed to dissent, was insulated from changes in popular opinion, and discriminated against women, young people, and racial minorities.

In addition to the dissatisfaction of the liberal wing of the party, the 1968 convention saw the culmination of discontent with the rules for selecting delegates. Since the first adoption of a strong civil rights plank, in the 1948 platform, there had been growing among party activists a desire to secure more adequate political representation for blacks, particularly on delegations from Southern states. Despite low rates of turnout, by 1952 black voters were sufficiently loyal to the Democratic Party to provide about 19 percent of the Democratic vote.[8] At the same time, the percentage of black delegates at national conventions had fallen substantially below both their percentage in the total population and their contribution to the Democratic vote.

At the 1964 Democratic convention, during the height of the civil rights movement, there was a major fight over the absence of blacks in the Mississippi delegation. The issue erupted again in 1968 over the seating of a racially mixed challenging delegation from Georgia. In both cases, Southern delegations were forced to accept black delegates. These disputes, however, surfaced in the Credentials Committee as challenges that were piecemeal, ad hoc, and transitory in nature.

Progress was grudgingly slow. Forcing two black delegates onto the 1964 all-white Mississippi delegation may be considered mere tokenism, but it took an enormous effort to accomplish. Even so, the Mississippi case had to be fought out again in 1968. In short, the history of Southern white intransigence forged a coalition of black and white delegates who sought ways of achieving massive change in one stroke, short-circuiting separate and sequential floor fights over each Southern state delegation.

During the 1960s and early 1970s, blacks were joined by other groups who were pressing for an expanded role in the political process. A resurgence of feminism in the country led to the formation of women's political organizations, as more women sought to run for office and serve in important campaign positions. The National Organization for Women was founded in 1966 by a group of activists including author Betty Friedan and Representative Martha Griffith. This organization was to press for enforcement of laws prohibiting sex discrimination, and in 1971 the National Women's Political Caucus was founded—through the efforts of Representatives Bella Abzug and Shirley Chisholm, Betty Friedan, and writer Gloria Steinem, among others. The NWPC was designed to involve more women in the political process. Young people, many motivated by opposition to the Vietnam War, also began to increase both their organizational capacity and their political demands. Many college students played important roles in the nomination campaigns of Senators Eugene McCarthy and Robert Kennedy in 1968, and George McGovern in 1972. Thus, the coalition pressing for change in 1968 had two thrusts: a desire to open convention procedures, and a drive to increase the representation of blacks, women, and young people.

The dissenters did not prevail on the issue of the 1968 presidential nomination, but their efforts at that convention did pave the way for some fundamental changes in the nomination process of the Democratic Party. By a narrow margin, the delegates approved a liberal minority report of the convention's Rules Committee. That report specified that the 1972 Convention Call would declare: "It is understood that a State Democratic Party, in selecting and certifying delegates to the National Convention, thereby undertakes a process in which all Democratic voters have had full and timely opportunity to participate."[9] In determining whether a state party had complied with this mandate, the national convention would require that "all feasible efforts have been made to assure that delegates are selected through Party primary, convention, or committee procedures open to public participation within the calendar year of the National Convention."[10]

In the spring of 1970, the Commission on Party Structure and Delegate Selection, headed by Senator McGovern,[11] produced its report. That report was a strong one, both in its critique of the 1968 delegate selection process and in its recommendations for change. With regard to the 1968 procedures, the commission concluded that "meaningful participation of Democratic voters in the choice of their presidential nominee was often difficult or costly, sometimes completely illusory, and, in not a few instances, impossible."[12] The commission found that more than a third of the convention delegates had, in effect, been selected before either the major campaign issues or the possible presidential candidates were known. In at least twenty states there were no rules (or, in the commission's judgment, inadequate ones) for selection of delegates, leaving it to the discretion of party leaders. And secret caucuses were found to be common at all levels of the process. Finally, the commission reported that the representation of blacks, women, and youth at the convention was substantially below the proportion of each group in the population.[13] (Blacks constituted 6 percent of the delegates and women 14 percent; in a majority of delegations, there was no more than a single delegate under 30 years of age.)

To remedy this, the commission recommended eighteen specific guidelines under which delegates to the 1972 convention should be selected. These guidelines can be broken into two groups, corresponding to the two sets of concerns that forged the coalition pushing for change both at the 1968 convention and within the reform commission. A list of procedural changes addressed the dissatisfaction of the liberal wing with the closed nature of the delegate selection process. A second group of guidelines responded to the desire for greater representation of blacks, women, and young people.

The first set of changes, those dealing with the procedures by which states select their delegates, was by far the most diverse and complex. Addressing the issue of timeliness, the commission recommended that the entire delegate selection process be conducted within the calendar year of the convention. And in an effort to ensure that selection be made more open, the commission recommended that state parties take the following steps: adopt explicit rules governing the process; forbid proxy voting; forbid use of the unit rule (which binds the whole delegation to the choice of the majority); require that, in all but rural areas, party meetings be held on uniform dates, at uniform times, and in public places of easy access; require "adequate" public notice of party meetings involving delegate selection.

To counteract inequities in group representation, the commission proposed that state parties "overcome the effects of past discrimination by affirmative steps to encourage representation on the National Convention delegations of minority groups, young people and women in reasonable relationship to their presence in the population of the state."[14] This group representation provision, which had been a focus of controversy since its enactment, was strengthened in 1971 by a rule interpretation made by Representative Fraser, McGovern's successor as commission chairman. In a letter to national party chairman Lawrence O'Brien, Fraser declared,

> We believe that state parties should be on notice that whenever the proportion of women, minorities, and young people in a delegation offered for seating in Miami [the convention site] is less than their proportion in the total population, and the delegation is challenged on the ground that [the group representation guidelines] were not complied with, such a challenge will constitute a *prima facie* showing of violation of the guidelines; and the State Democratic party has the burden of showing that the state party took full and affirmative action . . . to achieve such representation . . . and effective action.[15]

O'Brien passed the letter on to state chairmen and other party leaders. Congressman Fraser's interpretation, placing the burden of proof on challenged state party officials, appeared to confirm the suspicions of some of them that the new guidelines were in fact laying down quotas for racial minorities, women, and young people. These suspicions were to persist, even though the reform commission's report had stipulated, "It is the understanding of the Commission that [group representation] is not to be accomplished by the mandatory imposition of quotas."[16]

Somewhat to the surprise of both regulars and reformers within the party, compliance with the changes was widespread at state and local levels. Blacks, women, and young people, who had been severely underrepresented at the 1968 convention, increased their participation in 1972. The black delegates rose from 6 percent to 14 percent; women went from 14 to 36 percent; and youth (delegates under 30) increased from 2 percent to 23 percent. The openness provisions had an effect also, as state parties revised their rules to comply with the commission's recommendations.

We shall deal later in this book with the behavior of delegates at the Democratic national meetings that followed these rule changes. But it is important to note here that the rule changes significantly altered the demographic makeup of the convention and opened the selection process to wider participation.

The struggle over delegate selection rules in the Democratic Party has continued since 1972. In view of the opposition that the group representation "quota" rules engendered, it is not surprising that a new party delegate selection commission (headed by Baltimore city councilwoman Barbara Mikulski) recommended in late 1973 the abolition of the reasonable-representation guidelines. Instead, the commission's report put forward an "affirmative action" program to ensure participation by women, young people, and minority groups "as indicated by their presence in the Democratic electorate."[17] Although this language is very close to that in the McGovern Commission's report, the new guidelines did differ from the earlier ones in their standards for determining compliance. Under the Mikulski Commission's rules, which were adopted by the Democratic National Committee's executive committee in early 1974, compliance would not be determined by the presence of a "reasonable number" of youth, women, or minority delegates. Rather, the standard would be a vaguer one: a state party's efforts in encouraging participation by these groups.

Although the Mikulski Commission's guidelines became the delegate selection rules for the 1976 convention, the battle over rules and representation did not end with the adoption of those guidelines. For, pursuant to a vote of the 1972 convention, a unique party conference was held at Kansas City, Missouri, in December 1974. That conference was charged with the ratification of a formal charter to govern party affairs. Among the provisions of the charter were those concerning delegate selection at party conventions and conferences after 1976. As we shall see, the battles over "quotas," "affirmative action," and group representation were to erupt again at Kansas City.

Although our study is focused on the Democratic Party, where larger changes—and a greater degree of conflict—have taken place, it should be noted that the Republicans have also taken steps to alter their delegate selection and convention procedures. The 1968 Republican convention directed the appointment of a committee of the National Committee to consider ways of improving the convention process and implementing the party's rules against discrimination on the basis of race, religion, or national origin. The party's Committee on Delegates and Organization (referred to as the "DO Committee") was appointed in 1969.[18]

The committee, headed by Republican national committeewoman Rosemary Ginn of Missouri, reported its recommendations on delegate selection on July 1971. These recommendations called for open meetings held at various sites; bans on mandatory assessments of convention participants, proxy voting, and ex-officio delegates; an "endeavor" by each delegation to have an equal number of women and men; inclusion of persons under twenty-five years of age "in numerical equity to their voting strength" in each delegation; and doubling the size of convention committees to implement a new requirement for one person under twenty-five and one member of "a minority ethnic group," as well as one man and one woman, from each delegation.[19] At the 1972 Republican convention, the Rules Committee approved all the major DO Committee recommendations except those urging separate locations for state and district conventions and requiring representation for the young and minority groups.[20] The full convention ratified the Rules Committee's decisions.

The Analytical Questions Revisited

The turbulent changes in the Democratic Party's convention processes since 1968 add new dimensions—and increased importance—to the analytical questions we raised earlier. In studying party cleavages, for example, we are now confronted with a major rift in the Democratic Party between party regulars and the amateur activists whose participation grew out of concern about the Vietnam War, and whose entrance into party conventions was facilitated by the post-1968 reforms. Have these cleavages persisted, or are the different groups within the party growing closer together? And how do the various elements of the party differ in political style?

When we turn to collective decision making, we shall be particularly interested in the ways that newly-active groups—minorities, women, young people—have organized themselves to participate at party conventions. How effective are these groups in forming their own caucuses and how do such organizations change over time? The issue of demographic group representation has introduced important new questions for students of convention behavior.

Finally, the intensity of conflict within the Democratic Party poses obvious problems for legitimation and party unification. Under what conditions do delegates come to feel that the convention results are fair and worthy of support? How can convention losers come to support the results of the meeting?

The Study's Focus

This book focuses on the attitudes and behavior of delegates at the Democratic convention of 1972 and the party's special Charter Conference of 1974. Our data are drawn largely from our intensive studies of these party meetings. By comparing delegate attitudes and behavior in 1972 and 1974, we can gain an insight into the structure and evolution of party cleavages. And we can also deepen our understanding of how certain organizations—for example, group caucuses—change over time.

Besides offering two points in time for comparative purposes, the focus on these two party meetings serves another analytical function. As we shall see in Chapter 2, the charter conference—with its lack of a presidential nominating contest—presented natural experimental variations of some of the conditions we think crucial in explaining political behavior at the 1972 convention. Chapter 2 will identify recent trends in presidential nominations, summarize our conclusions about the 1972 convention, and put forward a set of propositions to be tested by the experience of the 1974 conference.

The next three chapters of the book are organized around the major analytical questions we have identified. In Chapter 3, after comparing the composition of the delegations in 1972 and 1974, we shall examine how the cleavage structure within the Democratic Party manifested itself at those two party gatherings. Then, in Chapter 4, we shall turn to the problem of decision-making arenas and the institutionalization of those arenas. In Chapter 5 we shall treat the crucial issue of legitimation of party convention decisions.

Having examined the empirical evidence on convention behavior, we shall go on to discuss the implications of our findings. Chapter 6 will focus on the implications for theories of party cleavage and reform, convention decision making, and legitimation. Chapter 7 will deal with the implications of our findings for the American political system in this time of institutional stress and change.

Notes

1. For an overview of the history of conventions, see V. O. Key, Jr., *Politics, Parties, and Pressure Groups* (5th ed.; New York: Crowell, 1964), pp. 396ff. The discussion here is based on Key's treatment.

2. S. E. Morison, "The First National Nominating Convention, 1808," *American Historical Review*, 17 (1912), 744–763. Quoted in Key, p. 397.

3. See Richard P. McCormick, "Political Development and the Second Party System," in W. N. Chambers and W. D. Burnham, eds., *The American Party Systems* (2nd ed.; New York: Oxford University Press, 1975), pp. 101–102.

4. One way in which political problems can be surmounted is through the development of formal institutions to contain potential conflicts. One author has defined political development in just this sense; see S. P. Huntington, *Political Order in Changing Societies* (New Haven: Yale University Press, 1968).

5. Key, p. 398.

6. See, for example, N. W. Polsby and A. B. Wildavsky, *Presidential Elections* (3rd ed.; New York: Scribner's, 1972), pp. 234–53; and Herbert McClosky, "Are Political Conventions Undemocratic?" *The New York Times Magazine*, August 4, 1968.

7. George McGovern, "The Lessons of 1968," *Harper's Magazine* (January 1970), p. 43.

8. The percentage of blacks voting for the Democratic national ticket in elections from 1952 to 1964 ran from 25 to 40 percent higher than the figures for the nation as a whole. See Robert Axelrod, "Where the Votes Come From: An Analysis of Electoral Coalitions, 1952–1968," *American Political Science Review*, 66 (January 1972), pp. 11–20.

9. Commission on Party Structure and Delegate Selection to the Democratic National Committee, *Mandate for Reform* (Washington, D.C., April 1970), p. 52.

10. Ibid.

11. Senator McGovern resigned from his position as commission chairman when he announced his presidential candidacy in June 1971; he was replaced by Minnesota congressman Donald Fraser.

12. *Mandate for Reform,* p. 3.

13. Ibid.

14. Ibid., pp. 12–13.

15. Letter from Rep. Fraser to Democratic National Chairman Lawrence O'Brien, November 29, 1971. Quoted in J. Lamond, *The Nominating Game in the Democratic Party: Delegate Selection and the Nominating Strategy.* Honors thesis, Government Department, Dartmouth College, 1974, p. 81.

16. *Mandate for Reform,* p. 24.

17. *Report of the Commission on Delegate Selection and Party Structure as Amended and Adopted by the Democratic National Committee's Executive Committee,* March 1, 1974.

18. For a review of reform developments within the Republican Party, see A. Ranney, "Changing the Rules of the Nominating Game," in J. D. Barber, ed., *Choosing the President* (Englewood Cliffs, N.J.: Prentice-Hall, 1974), pp. 85–86.

19. See R. C. Bain (rev. by J. H. Parris), *Convention Decisions and Voting Records* (2nd ed.; Washington, D.C.: Brookings, 1973), pp. 339–340.

20. Ibid., p. 340.

2 Changes in Presidential Nominating Conventions and Their Political Environment

This book is the second in a series of reports on the party nominating process. In our first study, on the 1972 Democratic convention, we had set out to test a number of standard hypotheses on nominating conventions, using the Miami Beach convention as our research site. We were particularly interested in the impact of the new reform rules and the effect of the increased numbers of blacks, women, and young people on convention processes.[1]

Two years later, there appeared a unique opportunity to extend the analysis developed in the 1972 study. The Democratic Party's Kansas City Charter Conference of 1974 presented us with natural experimental variations of some of the conditions we thought decisive in explaining the 1972 outcome. The absence of the presidential nominating contest, which imposes order upon election-year conventions, made the midterm meeting an excellent laboratory for the study of a fluid, dispersed bargaining situation. How do party cleavages make themselves felt in such a setting? How are decisions made? Which groups are important in initiating bargains and following through on them? How do these groups command the internal loyalty necessary for effective dealings with others? And when the party conference is over, how do various groups feel about the outcome, the party, and each other?

We hear much about brokered political conventions, at which delegates sit through multiple ballots to select a nominee. But in order to understand what the dynamics of a brokered convention would be under current conditions, we must look more closely at important political groups, the ways in which they organize themselves, and the ways in which they relate to each other.

In this chapter we shall review the 1972 experience and put forward a set of propositions based on our assessment of that experience and on our analysis of recent political history. Then we shall briefly outline our expectations of how those propositions would apply to the Kansas City conference.

Traditional Thinking about Convention Decision Making

To understand why the 1972 Democratic convention was expected to be such a sharp break with the past, it is important to bear in mind the classic model of convention decision making described in the political science literature. Historically, state delegations have been thought to be the key units for bargaining in conventions; operating under the unit rule, they bargain with each other and with candidate organizations.[2] The rank-and-file delegates are manipulated by hierarchical leaders holding important positions in national, state, or local party organizations.[3] In order to enhance their bargaining position, these leaders often try to stay uncommitted to any candidate until the moment that their endorsement is crucial to victory for the ultimate nominee. After the presidential balloting is over, the vice presidential nomination is awarded to a person whose selection will mollify those elements of the party who did not support the presidential choice. At the end of the convention, all groups rally around the ticket and the party receives a boost in starting the fall campaign.

The 1972 Experience

Certain rule changes made prior to the 1972 Democratic convention appeared to falsify some of the assumptions of the classic model. Because of the abolition of the unit rule and the requirements for opening up the delegate selection process, it was expected that hierarchical party leaders would have a harder time controlling the votes of a state delegation. Thus, the importance of such leaders in the bargaining process would be reduced. With decision-making power at the convention more widely dispersed, there would be an increase in the number of groups to be consulted, and this would strain an already burdened information system. Therefore, leaders would have strong incentives to find ways to assemble the smaller groups into more manageable bargaining units.

This expected need for new kinds of bargaining units appeared to coincide with the new forms of group representation at the convention. In 1972, it was clear that there would be increased convention participation by women, youth, and blacks. In the spring of that year, there were calls for black caucuses, women's caucuses, and youth caucuses—the formation of new arenas for bargaining.

Thus, in 1972 it appeared that convention decision making might conform to a somewhat different model, in which the importance of state delegations as arenas of decision would lessen and the need for new bargaining units would be met by the emergence of the new group caucuses. Before the convention began, both journalists and political activists expected the group caucuses to be important arenas of decision.[4] Our research in 1972 focused on these problems.

Summary of the 1972 Results

The results of that work, reported in D. Sullivan, J. Pressman, et al., *The Politics of Representation,* can be stated quite simply.[5] The efforts of the new groups to become autonomous powers in decision making were seriously undercut by (*a*) their inexperience in convention politics, (*b*) the hostility of the more traditional groups, (*c*) the organization of the convention, which favored traditional modes of participation, and (*d*) the cross-cutting cleavages that forced those most loyal to the new caucus groups to subordinate that loyalty to ensure George McGovern's nomination. Further, we observed that the shift in power toward the new groups brought about by McGovern's nomination neither made the McGovern supporters less purist nor the professional regulars more supportive. Rather, the regular professionals—seeing their preferred candidate defeated—adopted a decidedly more purist stance during the convention and, as a consequence, nullified the legitimating effects of McGovern's move toward the center. And finally, the conventions—for reasons discussed in *The Politics of Representation*—failed to rally the supporters of the defeated candidates around the winner.[6]

These results did not speak, however, to the more general problem of party conventions in a time of great social change. Was the McGovern movement, and the rules that aided it, an aberration soon forgotten in a return to normalcy or did it lie somewhere along an evolutionary path of party convention change? Clearly, the new groups in 1972 were not strong enough to deal a death blow to the classic model, even had they been so disposed. Yet their existence may have symbolized developments in American politics that will eventually transform the party convention system. Perhaps the anguished screams of party regulars over the new rules were misdirected, for the new rules may well be the surface symptoms of more profound changes. The classic model may be dying for reasons unrelated to the particulars of 1972. In the next section, we shall use our 1972 research to set down some of the major changes and their implications for the future of conventions.

Convention Behavior Reassessed: Some Propositions

Major changes of convention behavior have occurred in delegate decision making, political styles (purism vs. professionalism), arenas of decision, and the processes of legitimation.

(1) Delegates generally commit themselves to a candidate organization or functional group in the pre-convention period.

Since World War II the percentage of delegates committed to a candidate before coming to the convention has sharply increased.[7]

Five related factors—changes in delegate selection rules emphasizing primaries and reducing the number of ex-officio delegates; the reduced power of state and local parties; the growth of nationally based candidate organizations; the "surge" phenomena in which amateur activists are brought into presidential politics in large numbers; and a near monopoly of campaign funding by candidate organizations—have produced a "tipping" effect by which potential delegates find it increasingly in their interest to declare for a candidate early in the pre-convention period.

Most party people know that they must, if they are to be considered effective, become identified with a powerful group at the convention. Entering the convention arena as a state or local party member is no longer a feasible strategy. The nationalization of political arenas has eroded the feudal baronies of old party leaders. The capacity of candidate organizations to penetrate state and local constituencies has transformed the system. Their dominance is a consequence, in part, of their willingness to work in the pre-convention period; they are the only special-purpose organizations in the field developing statewide coalitions for their candidates.

Party and elected officials, if they are not part of the candidate organization vanguard, are usually busy with other things and, by necessity, become elements in the coalition plans of others. They are reduced to calculating gains and losses from joining alternative coalitions. In effect, the brokerage function formerly performed at the convention site has moved forward in time and is now represented by decisions to join one or the other candidate organizations.[8]

The effort by one candidate organization, as soon as it is taken seriously, to recruit delegates forces others to respond in kind. Potential candidates are forced to counterorganize if they are to have any chance at the nomination.[9] They can no longer wait to bargain with uncommitted party leaders because there will be too few of them to make a difference. The decline in the power of party leaders in presidential nominating politics has been accelerated by three related factors. First, national nominating politics is "surge" politics in the sense that large numbers of amateur activists are drawn into participation by candidate organizations.[10] Typically, as we shall show later, the ties of the amateur activist with candidate organizations, issue groups, or functional groups are strong; his ties with state and local parties are correspondingly weaker. If a party's nominating process is to be contested, the dynamics of competition will expand the scope of competition to include the amateur activist. If the delegate selection procedures are not biased against his representation, he will cut into the influence of party professionals. Second, there is the matter of money. New infusions of money, which alter the balance of power between state parties and candidate organizations, flow primarily to candidate organizations.[11] Parties themselves do not draw infusions of money in presidential years; the sweepstakes is among presidential aspirants, and they control the money. Third, and this hardly needs extended comment, state and local party organizations have atrophied in recent years.[12]

> (2) Delegate commitments to candidates or functional groups made in the pre-convention period last until it becomes apparent that the goal for which the commitment is made cannot be achieved in the course of the convention.

The strength of a delegate's commitment to a candidate group is a direct function of the amount of psychological or behavioral work done by the delegate in the pre-convention period. The delegate's investment of time and resources before the convention is irrevocable; thus he is strongly disposed to find ways of behaving that are consistent with his original commitment.[13] For most, the basic reason for being a delegate at nominating convention is to express one's commitment for a candidate; other purposes are important but secondary. Delegates have arranged the elements in their belief system before arriving at the convention site. For example, many women delegates to the 1972 convention had arrived at a conclusion concerning the relationship of their chosen candidate to women's goals; what happened during their stay in Miami seemed not to disturb the arrangement. For the short time that delegates are at conventions, they are more interested in learning how to behave in a manner consistent with their commitments than in acquiring information that might alter them. Political conventions are not very good places for deep thought about prior decisions concerning means and ends. When a functional group competes with a candidate organization for delegate loyalty, the delegate may feel much less cross-pressured than may be imagined, for he has usually made a commitment in favor of the candidate organization. In this way, in 1972, the wind was taken out of the sails of the various caucus movements before they really got under way.

Other factors are also important. If, for example, a convention is deadlocked, attention usually turns to a compromise candidate. If a conclusion is reached that none of the front runners can obtain a majority, the prior commitment of the delegate to a most favored candidate is psychologically released, and he becomes amenable to a reconsideration of the relationship between group caucus goals and his choice of candidate. When this happens we would expect the relative importance of candidate organizations to decline. There is yet another factor—the expectation of victory in the election subsequent to the nomination. For most delegates the expectation of victory in the November election is a conditional one: victory depends on a unified party moving into the electoral phase of the struggle. This conditional expectation acts as an incentive, heightening the salience and importance of party unity in the nomination phase. Most delegates, convinced that a unified party can win, avoid disruptive behavior during the convention. This tends to cement their decision to subordinate their identification with interest groups—labor, blacks, women, youth, and so on—to identification with the candidate organization. If, on the other hand, expectation of victory begins to fade, the delegates might reconsider prior commitments, and work for other goals.

> (3) Purist political styles predispose delegates to strong affiliations with candidate organizations or functional groups at the convention.

The emergence of the conflict between issue-oriented (ideologically pure) and party-oriented activists in the 1960s has been noted by a number of scholars of political parties.[14] James Q. Wilson, in his book on the emergence of amateur Democratic clubs in three cities in the late 1950s, was probably the first scholar to give the problem sustained theoretical attention. Wilson's analysis revealed a recurring conflict between Democratic regulars and issue-oriented amateurs. In his view, the issue orientations of the amateurs were connected, not to self or narrow group interest, but to a larger public interest. For the amateur, participation in politics became an extension of private morality into the public sector. Aaron Wildavsky, in his commentary on Goldwater supporters at the 1964 Republican convention, applied the notion of purists and politicians to nominating politics. Wildavsky used the distinction between purists and professional politicians in much the same way Wilson did for the amateur and regular Democrats. Wildavsky pursued the purist-versus-politician theme in his study of the 1968 Democratic convention, casting the young McCarthyites in the role of purists and the Humphrey supporters in the role of professionals.[15] Soule and Clarke, in another study of the same convention, developed a measure of purism or, as they called it, amateurism, that clearly distinguished McCarthy and Humphrey delegates.[16] Purism was not, then, solely a rightist phenomenon. It described leftist McCarthyites in 1968 as well as rightist Goldwaterites in 1964.

In 1972, the McGovern surge in the primaries and state conventions again brought the themes of purism and reform to the surface of political conflict. As in 1968, the conflict between the regulars and the insurgents led by McGovern was as much a clash of styles as it was conflict over policy.

If we compare the attitudes of the purists and professional politicians toward the major functions of nominating conventions— the selection of a candidate, the writing of a party platform, and the resolution of political differences—we can gain a clearer perspective on the distinction between purists and professionals. Purists pledge themselves to a candidate on the basis of his stand on the issues; professionals justify their commitment in terms of the candidate's capacity to unify the party and win elections. For professionals, issue preferences are relevant but secondary. Concerning the writing of a platform—the second major function of nominating conventions—the purist arrives at a platform that is correct according to some conception of the public interest or good; for the professional a platform is correct if it placates the losers without alienating the winners and, at the same time, offers a good chance of winning the general election.

Finally, for the purists, the resolution of issue differences ought to occur through open discussion and debate in which each participant has an equal weight; for the professional, issue differences are resolved through bargaining and compromise in which the outcome is determined (and should be) by the relative power of contending groups. For the purists, intra-party democracy is highly valued; for the professionals it is not.

Because purists are so single minded politically, they tend to put their political eggs in one basket—the organization of the candidate to whom they have committed themselves. Yet if their candidate waffles on the issues they grow uneasy at his departure from a correct position. Professionals, on the other hand, have commitments to party as well as to issues. They tend to view issues as instruments for fashioning majorities, not as ends in themselves. But the matter of political style is more complicated than we have indicated. Let us now turn to its other determinants.

(4) Political style is partly a function of personal characteristics of the delegates—length of involvement in party affairs, age, class, background, and so on—but it varies according to the organizational situations in which the delegates find themselves.

It has been widely assumed that McGovern delegates, who dominated the 1972 convention, were ideological activists who were unwilling to compromise in the interests of party unity and victory in November. Supporters of the "regular" candidates, who controlled the 1968 convention (and earlier ones) but lost out in 1972, are seen as pragmatic professional types who put the interests of party and electoral victory over those of ideological purity. Thus it is argued that the 1972 convention represented a sharp—and disturbing—break with the traditions of conducting party business.

It would be a mistake, however, to divide the 1972 convention too neatly into camps of purist and professional, and to argue that the convention itself constituted a radical break with the past. Although it is unquestionably true that McGovern delegates had many purist attributes, our evidence showed that these people were also willing to compromise repeatedly to advance the interests of their candidate. As in previous conventions, delegates directed their behavior toward the nomination of their preferred candidate rather than toward the expression of group interest through identification with special group causes. In this way, their behavior conformed to patterns of decision making observed in other conventions. Finally, there is some evidence that the "regular" delegates took on some purist attributes of their own in the course of the convention.

The evidence gleaned from the 1972 Democratic convention

raises some serious questions about the assertion that the dominant group of delegates there were uncompromising ideologues who wrested control of the party from their pragmatic, party-regular opponents and changed the nature of the convention process itself. Interviews and other data show that: McGovern delegates were willing to yield on ideological purity when it would help their candidate's prospects in the convention and election; the McGovern delegates did not extend the notion of compromise to the events following the nomination (they resumed a more purist stance); despite some observers' expectations of sharp changes, the decision-making patterns and arenas at the 1972 convention were similar to those of the past; and the supporters of "regular" candidates actually developed a purist orientation in the course of the convention.

Our conclusions suggest a modification of the theory of purism and professionalism. First, purists in one arena are not necessarily purists in another arena. When members of the McGovern coalition dealt with each other, accommodation and compromise were the order of the day. When the arena shifted from the nomination of McGovern to the issue of party unity, many McGovernites became purists. That is, they saw little need to promote party unity. Second, the regulars were far more supportive of accommodation and compromise as long as the nominee would be one of "theirs." As soon as it became apparent that McGovern was going to win, many regulars shed their professional attitudes and donned purist ones. One might argue that the change in style was a rational choice for the regulars but not for the purists. But even if that point is granted, it is still important to bear in mind that political style — purist or professional — is often a rational response to one's situation. The maintenance of a purist stance by many of the McGovernites still testifies, of course, to the power of the notion of political style as a persisting orientation toward political events.

(5) If in a convention described by conditions (1–4) no majority occurs on the first ballot, bargaining among leaders will break down.

We have argued that once it becomes clear to a delegate that the group with which he is principally identified cannot achieve its goal, he will turn his attention to his next most powerful group.

For the more amateur purists, this means an increasing responsiveness to issues and functional interest groups—blacks, women, and so on. In that case, leaders of candidate organizations may be able to release the votes of their delegates but will be unable to deliver them; it should be equally difficult for amateur purists of the left or right.

The rising salience of functional groups and the inclusion of their leaders as bargainers will alienate those delegates most committed to traditional modes of participation in party affairs—state and local party structures. Unless the candidate selected as a consequence of such bargaining has a firm footing in the more traditional section of the party, disaffection of the party professionals will result. And conversely, a candidate of the party professionals will not gain acceptance without a strong constituency in the new groups.

Thus a convention in which there are large numbers of delegates with strong prior commitments and reasonably strong issue differences, the prospects for legitimation at the convention are dim at best.

Propositions Applied to the 1974 Kansas City Conference

At first glance, it might seem impossible for a party as sharply divided as the Democrats have been to hold a convention without suffering an outbreak of sustained hostility. But at the Democratic Charter Conference in 1974, the delegates did not engage in the hostile behavior that some observers had predicted.[17] The fact that the party was able to come together as successfully as it did in Kansas City is both a tribute to the delegates and an indicator of the rather peculiar conditions that prevailed there.

A strange mixture of the old and new would be present at Kansas City; some factors wuld promote the resurgence of the classic mode of convention bargaining while others would enhance the newly won power of caucus groups. In the light of the propositions we set forth earlier, let us now review some of the expectations we had about delegate behavior in 1974.

First, we anticipated that the composition of the delegates at Kansas City would differ substantially from Miami. A party charter is an internal party affair and thus should attract active office holders in the party organization and others more strongly identified with the party. Second, we thought a more pronounced concern with party would dampen the move toward walkouts, or other forms of behavior perceived as disruptive or "non-integrative" by the mainstream delegates. Because of the conference's concern with organizational issues, many of the reformers attracted to Kansas City would be susceptible to appeals for party unity. Thus the stereotyped view of reformer vs. establishment would be even less accurate than it had been in the past. Third, because the charter provisions would not take effect until 1980, the politics of the 1976 presidential nomination would have little effect on the Kansas City proceedings, in shaping either political behavior or attitudes toward charter issues.

Fourth, our 1972 research had indicated that the weaker the candidate organizations, the stronger the influence of the group caucuses. Thus we anticipated that 1974 would see far more effective caucus efforts, especially by blacks and women.

Fifth, not only would the absence of powerful candidate organizations facilitate caucus unity, but two years had elapsed since the caucuses had attempted to influence the outcome in Miami in 1972. The organizational learning that went on between 1972 and 1974 would add, we thought, to the effectiveness of the caucuses at Kansas City.

Sixth, the absence of powerful candidate organizations, recruiting and educating delegates, plus the complexity of the charter provisions meant that most delegates came to Kansas City with rather weak commitments to most charter provisions but with a diffuse desire to see the charter through in the name of party unity. The lack of information on the part of delegates plus the ambiguity surrounding charter provisions would allow ample opportunity for group or party leaders not only to arrange compromises but to get their followers to accept them.

Seventh, the willingness of delegates to compromise would be buttressed by their belief that Watergate and the declining economy had conspired to make the Democratic Party a likely winner in the next presidential election.

Finally, increased willingness to compromise, on the part of the more purist delegates, might have come from two more years' experience of working with the party.

Research Design

In 1972 we had limited ourselves to interviewing delegates during the convention; in 1974 we decided to supplement our interviews over the three-day period with mailed pre- and post-conference questionnaires. Thus we would have three points in time for examining changes in perceptions and attitudes. As soon as delegate lists became available to us in November 1974, we mailed out our pre-conference questionnaire to a random sample of 460 delegates; 284 (62 percent) returned the questionnaire before the conference opened. An additional twenty questionnaires were returned after the conference; they were excluded from our analysis. At the conference we interviewed a random sample of 165 delegates drawn from the initial sample of 460 delegates. We were able to complete 145 (85 percent) of our interviews. Finally, after the conference we drew an additional sample including all those who had completed the pre-convention questionnaire. Of the 344 questionnaires mailed out, 182 (53 percent) were returned. The response rate did seem a bit low, so we checked the composition of the pre-convention sample against that of the post-convention. The only statistically significant difference concerned representation of blacks. It had dropped substantially in the post-convention sample.

Our questionnaires, as well as our interview form, were designed to explore the delegates' conceptions of (1) their roles at Kansas City, (2) where the important decisional arenas would be, (3) which groups or institutions would be (or had been) most powerful at the conference, and (4) their attitudes toward the charter issues and major participants. We tried as much as possible to phrase pre- and post-conference questions in the same words. The questionnaires are included here as appendixes. For the most part, our questions continued the inquiry we had begun in our work on the 1972 Democratic convention. To supplement the question-naires, members of our research team observed meetings of state delegations and group caucuses (of women, blacks, labor delegates, and so forth). We also made use of access to the floor of the con-ference to talk to delegates and observe the activities of various groups. Thus our data consist of written questionnaires, oral inter-views, and observations of convention activity itself.

Now that we have reviewed some important recent changes in convention behavior and introduced our study, let us move to an examination of our empirical results.

Notes

1. Our work is reported in D. G. Sullivan, J. L. Pressman, B. I. Page, and J. J. Lyons, *The Politics of Representation: The Democratic Convention 1972* (New York: St. Martin's, 1974), and in J. L. Pressman and D. G. Sullivan, "Convention Reform and Conventional Wisdom: An Empirical Assessment," *Political Science Quarterly*, vol. 89, no. 3 (Fall), 1974, pp. 539–562.

2. The Democratic unit rule required that the entire vote of a state delegation be cast as the majority of the delegation desired, if the state delegation had been so instructed by the state convention.

3. For further discussion of this model, see P. T. David, R. M. Goldman, and R. C. Bain, *The Politics of National Party Conventions* (Washington, D.C.: Brookings, 1959); N. W. Polsby and A. B. Wildavsky, "Uncertainty and Decision-Making at the National Conventions," in N. W. Polsby, R. A. Dentler and P. A. Smiths, eds., *Politics and Social Life* (Boston: Houghton Mifflin, 1963); and N. W. Polsby and A. B. Wildavsky, *Presidential Elections* (3rd ed.; New York: Scribner's, 1972).

4. For example, see "Caucus Calling Meeting July 9 of Black Democratic Dele-gates," *New York Times*, June 14, 1972.

5. *The Politics of Representation.* Chapter 3 deals with the new group arenas, Chapter 4 with the platform, and Chapter 5 with political style.

6. Ibid., pp. 127–132.

7. J. Lamond, *The Nominating Game in the Democratic Party: Delegate Selection and the Nominating Strategy.* Honors thesis, Government Department, Dartmouth College, 1974.

8. For a standard treatment see A. Wildavsky and N. Polsby, *Presidential Elections.*

9. E. E. Schattschneider, *Party Government* (New York: Holt, Rinehart and Winston, 1942).

10. See E. G. DeFelice, *Pre-Convention Politics: The Surge of Amateur Delegates from Illinois, 1972.* Paper delivered at the 1974 American Political Science Associ-ation Meeting, Chicago, Illinois, September 2.

62189

11. On funding of candidate organizations, see A. Wildavsky and N. Polsby, *Presidential Elections.*

12. W. D. Burnham, *Critical Elections and the Mainsprings of American Politics* (New York: Norton, 1971).

13. Investment of political resources is a form of prior commitment treated most interestingly in J. W. Brehm and A. R. Cohen, *Explorations in Cognitive Dissonance* (New York: Wiley, 1962).

14. A. Wildavsky, "The Goldwater Phenomenon: Purists, Politicians, and the Two-Party System," *Review of Politics,* 27 (July 1965), pp. 386–413, and J. Q. Wilson, *The Amateur Democrat* (Chicago: University of Chicago Press, 1966). See especially Chapter 12, "The New Party Politics: An Appraisal."

15. A. Wildavsky, "The Meaning of 'Youth' in the Struggles for Control of the Democratic Party," in A. Wildavsky, *The Revolt Against the Masses* (New York: Basic Books, 1971), pp. 270–287.

16. J. Soule and J. Clarke, "Amateurs and Professionals: A Study of Delegates to the 1968 Democratic National Convention," *American Political Science Review,* 64 (September 1970), pp. 888–889.

17. See "Divided Democrats Face New Bloodbath," *Boston Evening Globe,* August 19, 1974; C. Lydon, "Divided Democrats Face Major Fight at Charter Convention in Kansas City," *New York Times,* October 16, 1974; and A. L. Otten, "Squabbling Democrats May Widen Their Rifts at Charter Session," *Wall Street Journal,* December 2, 1974.

Reform Issues and Party Cleavages

The Democrats' 1974 Charter Conference was a unique event in American political history. It was the first time that a U.S. political party had held a midterm meeting of this kind. And the charter ratified at the converence was the first formal constitution ever adopted by a major American party. Therefore, it is important to review what the most significant issues were in drawing up the charter; the examination will highlight some of the current disputes over party reform.

Going beyond the development of the charter and its substantive provisions, we shall use our study of the conference to examine continuing developments within the Democratic Party. By focusing both on the delegate selection process and on the attitudes of delegates at the conference, we can gain insight into the structure of relationships among the party's component groups. By comparing our 1974 findings with comparable data from 1972 (as well as with available records from 1968), we can assess developments within the party over time.

The Making of the Charter: Some Contested Issues

In the year before the 1972 convention, two commissions of the national Democratic Party—the Commission on Delegate Selection and Party Rules chaired by Congressman Donald Fraser (after George McGovern resigned to run for the Presidency), and the Commission on Convention Rules headed by Congressman James O'Hara—met in joint session to draft a proposed charter for the party to be submitted to the 1972 national convention. Compared to the seemingly more important changes in those years in procedures for selecting delegates to national conventions, the charter received little attention and little political support. Just prior to the 1972 convention, in an accommodation reached between Senator McGovern and congressional leaders troubled by many of the proposed articles, a substitute resolution was offered in place of the charter. That resolution, which was passed in an uproar on the last night of the convention, established a new commission to hold hearings and write another charter draft, and mandated a national "conference"[1] to ratify the document.

During 1973 and 1974, the Charter Commission met under the chairmanship of Terry Sanford, former governor of North Carolina. The most important of the provisions contained in the charter's twelve articles can be summarized in three broad categories. First, the document distributes power among the various national institutions of the party: the national convention, the national committee, and its executive committee and chairperson. These provisions did little more than enshrine operating procedures that are adequately described in the available literature.[2]

A second set of provisions envisioned the construction of strong new centralized party structures; if passed in the form desired by the more ardent reformers, these provisions would have indeed embodied important political change. Four new organizational units were established by the final document: a Judicial Council, a National Finance Council, a National Education and Training Council, and the possibility of holding future conferences at the mid-point of a presidential term. For each of these, the independence, flexibility, and breadth of the mandate provided by the charter enacted at Kansas City fell short of the goals of those who had initially proposed such institutions. Those actors, however, could content themselves with the possibility of an incremental expansion of the strength of these new institutions.

The third major area of legislation in Kansas City, and the issue that drew most of the energies of the participants, concerned the principles of participation and representation in party processes and structures. In 1972, the guidelines regulating delegate selection so as to provide representation for different social groups (principally minorities, women, and youth) were bitterly denounced by many conservative Democrats as mandating a quota system for these groups.[3] Since 1972, this arrangement has been replaced by programs of affirmative action in both the charter and the delegate selection rules for 1976. Rather than focusing upon the *results* of the delegate selection procedures, the new approach to providing adequate representation to traditionally disadvantaged groups places emphasis upon reaching out to involve those groups in the *process* by which delegates are selected. The language specifying the extent and nature of these affirmative action programs became the focal point of the climatic political struggle at Kansas City.[4]

Three key points were strenuously debated during the preconference period: (1) Should affirmative action plans be required in "all party affairs" (Article X, Section 3) and what meaning should be attached to that phrase? (2) Should certain social groups be specifically targeted for programs designed to encourage their participation (also X.3)? (3) If a state party has carried out an approved affirmative action program, should its delegation be liable to challenge on the sole basis of social composition, and, if so, who should bear the burden of proof in such challenges (Article X.6)?

Article X.6 became the most contested issue of the conference, probably because it defined how close to or distinct from a quota system the new procedures were to be. In 1972, the implication of the McGovern Commission guidelines was that composition did constitute a basis for challenging credentials and that the challenged delegation bore the burden of proof that its composition had not resulted from discrimination.[5] Article X.6 went through numerous revisions before a version reached the floor that had been borrowed directly from a negotiated compromise in the rules governing delegate selection in 1976. National Chairman Robert Strauss, the Democratic governors, and several labor unions had endorsed this wording, which the Women's and Black Caucuses found unacceptable.[6] On the other hand, the AFL-CIO leadership, particularly George Meany and Alexander Barkan (the head of labor's Committee on Political Education), had so many problems with other sections of Article X that a retention of Section 6 was seen as a precondition for accepting the entire charter. Barkan threatened to walk out if X.6 were taken out; the Black Caucus threatened to do the same if it were left in. Only a last-minute compromise saved the conference from a walkout by either side.

The debate over X.6 was a singular and climactic focus for most delegate behavior. In fact, the struggle engaged so much of the available organizational resources that many other issues, which James MacGregor Burns argued would ultimately prove more profound for the future of the party, were buried through inattention.[7] Yet, in spite of the conference's central focus on X.6, most of the delegates we interviewed stated that the word changes gained by the Women's and Black Caucuses were really quite trivial in their *effects upon* the delegate selection and credentials challenge processes. In fact, the importance of the Kansas City conference stems not so much from the language of the charter adopted as from the political processes that took place before and during the conference.

Delegate Selection Procedures and Results

Delegates were selected for the Kansas City conference through formal procedures and institutions similar to those of national conventions: caucus systems, state conventions, state committees, and primaries. Unlike the case of delegate selection for national conventions, however, state parties were not bound to comply with state law. They were free, therefore, to write new *party* law for this new, and possibly unique, institution. Only eight states turned to primaries; most opted for a combination of tiered caucuses on the Congressional district level and state committee selection of the at-large delegations.

While on the surface the formal procedures used in 1974 may appear similar to those leading to national conventions, there was a noteworthy difference. Because delegate selection was not organized by competing candidate organizations, there was an absence of the "glue" provided by organized candidate preference across state delegations; thus, local party structures emerged as perhaps the only organized forces equipped to compete in the vacuum. Two coalition groups—the liberal Democratic Planning Group (DPG) and the more conservative Coalition for a Democratic Majority (CDM)—attempted with little success to perform the functions of candidate organizations at nominating conventions.

The issue of delegate selection rules for the Charter Conference did not produce the same degree of interest that was generated over the 1972 rules. Generally, advocates of openness in party structures argue that the policy implications of a presidential nominating process are so important that delegate selection mechanisms should be open to, indeed should actively *encourage*, participation by all Democratic voters. While reformers like Alan Baron, the national director of DPG, would never argue that the processes for Kansas City should be closed to all but party cadres and activists, the question of broad social representation did not become a political issue then as it did in 1972. Baron and CDM's director Penn Kemble agreed that Kansas City was essentially an internal party affair.

Still, the increase in the number of party professionals from 1972 to 1974 was startling (see Table 3.1). Although we expected the charter convention to attract those involved in party affairs, we were somewhat surprised to find the percentage of party office holders five times as high in 1974 as in either 1968 or 1972. Consistent with this finding, Table 3.1 shows a sharp increase from

Table 3.1 Changes in political experience of convention delegates from 1968 to the 1974 Kansas City convention*

	HOLD PARTY OFFICE	HOLD EFFECTIVE OFFICE	WERE DELEGATES AT PRIOR CONVENTIONS	IDENTIFY STRONGLY WITH DEMOCRATIC PARTY
1968	14%	18%	34%	—
1972	14%	17%	16%	63%
1974	70%	31%	31%	88%

*The 1968 data are from John E. Schofield, *1968 Presidential Nominating Convention*, Project IMPRESS. The 1972 data are from CBS and D. Sullivan et al., *The Politics of Representation* (New York: St. Martins, 1974). The 1974 data are from our questionnaires. The Kansas City project was based on a sample of elected, not ex-officio, delegates.

The party identification question is almost identical to the standard University of Michigan Survey Research Center question. In 1972 it was asked orally; in 1974 it was on mailed pre-convention and post-convention questionnaires.

1972 to 1974 in the percentage of strong party identifiers (63 to 88 percent) as well as a substantial increase in the percentage of delegates with prior convention experience. In addition, a large and important contingent of voting delegates (approximately 17 percent) were seated ex-officio by virtue of holding high party or public office (governors, congressmen, national committeepersons).

Although not a major issue, political representation of various social categories was an important theme in the process of delegate selection and—as the affirmative action provision—stirred up the major dispute at the conference itself. The National Women's Political Caucus was particularly active in pushing for female delegates. But the NWPC could not place anyone on a delegation in the same way that candidate organizations can; women fought their own way onto delegations, albeit aided by continual pressure from state and national organizations.

If selection as a delegate in 1974 is an indicator of political strength, then women have come into their own as an important center of power within the party. Table 3.2 indicates that the gains scored by women at the 1972 convention were not lost by the removal of quotas; the percentage of women delegates did not drop at all. The percentage of young delegates (we have counted as "young" those thirty-four years of age or less) fell to a level midway between 1968 and 1972, the year in which the insurgent McGovern movement mobilized large numbers of youth and rewarded them with delegate positions. In the absence of quotas, and without candidate organization support, the young as a political grouping did not have sufficient power to command access to the conference. If youth were to participate at Kansas City it would be as blacks, women, party regulars, and so on. But if the convention was socially

Table 3.2 Changes in social background of convention delegates, from the 1968 Democratic convention to the 1974 Kansas City convention*

	Age Over 34	White	Male	Completed College	Law Degree
1968	88%	94%	86%	61%	31%
1972	62%	80%	64%	58%	29%
1974	73%	87%	64%	70%	21%

*For sources see note to Table 3.1.

representative by certain selected criteria, it certainly did nothing to dispel the belief that party elites are essentially middle to upper class in social background. In fact, the percentage of delegates who had completed college rose from 58 percent in 1972 to 70 percent in 1974, a level exceeding that of 1968 (61 percent). Yet those who feel that lawyers are overrepresented in party elites may find some small satisfaction in their continued decline (Table 3.2).

Thus the 1974 delegates at Kansas City were politically more experienced (as measured by party office holding and elective office holding), than their counterparts in either 1968 or 1972, better educated (although with fewer lawyers), and far more strongly identified with the Democratic Party than in 1972. But what is even more important, the gap between the McGovernites and the Democratic regulars seemed to be narrowing; in political and social profile they were more alike. Delegates who supported McGovern in 1972 were just as likely to be party office holders as were Humphrey supporters, and just a little less likely to hold elective office.

The Evolution of Political Cleavages, 1968–1974: Some Hypotheses

During recent years, much has been said about the deep cleavages that exist within the Democratic Party. Often, the contending sides in the struggle are portrayed as "liberal-amateur-purist-reformers" on one side and "conservative-professional-pragmatic-anti-reformers" on the other. But can we be more precise as to the nature of the cleavages and contending groups within the party? Which groups and individuals within the party cluster together? On what dimensions do the groups differ? On what dimensions are they similar? Are the cleavages within the party getting deeper with time, or are previously antagonistic groups coming together? Let us turn now to the closely related issues of party rule reform and party cleavages.

Many of the delegates at Kansas City had been present at Chicago in 1968 (15 percent) and at Miami in 1972 (32 percent). The Charter Conference was a continuation of the battle for control of the Democratic Party and, as such, might be expected to reawaken the passions of those who had fought each other in 1968 and 1972. Most delegates at Kansas City had supported either a "regular" candidate in 1972 (51 percent for Muskie, Humphrey, or Jackson) or the insurgent McGovern candidacy (33 percent).

The battles in both 1968 and 1972 spilled over the substantive issues of Vietnam, race, women, and nomination politics into the issue of party reform. Those who had supported, for example, an anti-war candidate in 1968 argued for party reform. The 1974 reform issues, transformed into draft charter provisions, were the same issues concerning intra-party democracy that had so animated discussions in 1968 and 1972.

The cause of reform had been first taken up by the defeated McCarthy supporters in 1968; frustrated by their failure to take over the party, they were quick to chastise regulars for conducting a convention that violated fundamental democratic norms. Most were amateur activists drawn into participation by the issues of Vietnam and race. Many remained active in politics after 1968 and came to Miami in 1972 as supporters of George McGovern. In 1972 the losers of 1968 had become winners and felt that a new era of intra-party democracy had begun. And many thought that their new constituency strategy would, if successful, reduce the importance of the regular's contribution to electoral success. But as we pointed out in *The Politics of Representation,* party regulars dissociated themselves from the McGovern electoral effort—thinking it doomed to failure—and waited to pick up the pieces after the election.[8]

Intense political struggles frequently call into question the legitimacy of the rules under which they take place. Losers, discontent with their lot, seek rule changes that will increase their chances of success in future battles. Thus the insurgent McCarthyites challenged the legitimacy of the rules under which they had lost, and succeeded in bringing about reform. In 1972 the regulars lost and demanded changes that they thought fair and that would improve their chances in the next round.

Internal party politics may be peculiarly susceptible to conflicts over rules; nominating conventions meet only once every four years. The meetings usually take place under changed political circumstances, with new issues and new candidates. Rules for delegate selection and convention decision making—having no special place in anyone's ideal democracy—are viewed more instrumentally, as helping or hurting particular candidates. A faction gaining the upper hand in the party will often reinterpret or rewrite the rules to favor its preferred candidate. And as control of the party fluctuates between factions, so do the rules that codify its procedures. The normal restraints on tampering with the rules are either absent or weakened; conventions are not, after all, continuing bodies in which the maintenance of and respect for rules is of great importance.

As long as contending factions alternate in control of the party and are not too far apart on the issues, such rule tampering does no fundamental damage. It does not even reduce the convention's capacity to legitimate a particular outcome. For legitimation is more dependent on the vital interests of the losers being satisfied than on the niceties of procedure.

But as issue conflicts intensify with the entry of amateur activists, fights over rules take on a different significance. For the regulars, who share a common set of assumptions about politics and their own roles, are now challenged by amateur activists whose political style is more issue oriented and who view politics as an opportunity for moral exhortation. The issues are so deeply felt that the combination of issue and style difference is an explosive one. It may lead to what Seymour Martin Lipset has referred to as a developmental crisis in the party.[9] Sharp differences in policy orientation are coupled with challenges to the legitimacy of the rules under which decisions are made. Such crises subside only when views on issues cease to be linked closely with questions of the legitimacy of the rules.

For the amateur activist, issue positions signal one's moral worth; those who oppose the correct position are not only wrong, they are immoral. The amateur activist's urge to transform political discourse into a morality play runs against the grain of the party regulars who have learned to separate their own private moral convictions from the public positions they take in the name of the party. For the amateur activist, party is little more than a vehicle for the articulation of a correct issue position. If in their eyes its rules prevent the articulation of a correct position or the nomination of the correct candidate, then the rules that allow such an immoral outcome must be undemocratic, and thus must be changed. The logic of their belief system compels them to reject the legitimacy of party rules that allowed such an outcome. The orientation of the amateur activist, which we have called a purist style in *The Politics of Representation*, couples *pro-reform* with *anti-party* attitudes.[10]

Most party regulars, those who have been active in party affairs for a long time and have a strong identification with party, pride themselves on a professional as opposed to a purist approach to issues and organization. The rules the purist sees as undemocratic the regular sees as protecting the party from a takeover by those who would change its function from a political party to an ideological interest group. Whereas the purist values party only as a device for articulating issue positions, the professional identifies emotionally with the party and sees it as a means for achieving his political goals—winning elections and influencing public policy. We have called this political style professional because it couples *pro-party* and *anti-reform* attitudes. The logic of the professional's beliefs compelled him in 1968 to see the purist demands for party reform (*a*) as showing the amateurs' lack of commitment to party, (*b*) as an attack on the regulars' power position, and (*c*) as evidence of the non-professional (and thus anti-professional) attitudes of the purist amateurs.

In Figure 3.1 we have graphed the basic dimensions of the conflict; the vertical axis represents the pro-party/anti-party dimension and the horizontal axis the pro-reform/anti-reform one. If our thinking is correct on the nature of the conflict between regulars and amateurs, in the early stages the amateurs should be located in the lower right quadrant (anti-party and pro-reform) and the regulars in the upper left quadrant (anti-reform and pro-party). The issues, leaders, and groups in such a polarized situation should fall somewhere along the line (purism-professionalism) extending from the lower right to the upper left quadrant (from a purist to a professional style). In this stage (we shall call this Stage I in the remainder of the chapter), attitudes towards issues, groups, and party decision-making procedures go together. The delegate's location on the single purist-professional continuum allows us to deduce his attitudes towards reformers (McCarthy, McGovern), reform groups (Black and Women's Caucus), issues (Vietnam), the regulars (LBJ, Humphrey), and the party.

The Stage I model may describe accurately the ways in which regulars and reformers thought about each other when the former had power and the latter sought it. But the new purists did get a chance to exercise party power through McGovern's nomination and their own accession to party offices during and after the elec-

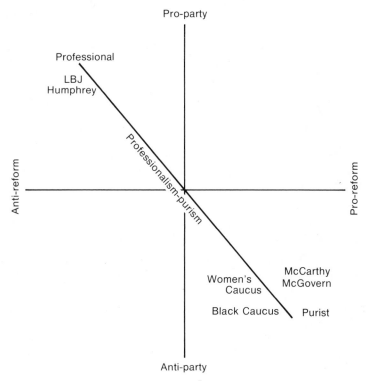

Figure 3.1
Stage I (1968–1972). In this simple conception, delegates like those located in their own quadrant and dislike those located in the opposite quadrant.

tion. Although success did not modify their levels of purism at the convention in 1972, as we showed in *The Politics of Representation*, continued participation as party office holders from 1972 to 1974 might.[11] As their purism lessened (or their professionalism grew), their pro-reform posture might not dictate strong anti-regular attitudes. And the regulars, who had become more purist in 1972 in the sense that their concern with issue purity grew as they lost power to the McGovernites, might become more accommodating as they worked with new activists in the party. In this way, attitudes toward reform might become detached from attitudes toward party, and cleavages would cease to form along the purist-professional axis.

In the next section, we shall take a closer look at the attitudes reformers and regulars had toward themselves and each other in

1972 and 1974. Our goal will be to examine the validity of the Stage I model as a description of 1972 and, if accurate for 1972, its validity for 1974. The analysis is a bit complicated by the fact that 1972 was a nominating convention and 1974 a charter convention. Some of the observed change may have been due to the fact that a charter convention can build consensus in a way that a nominating convention cannot. Although we shall deal more fully with this problem in Chapter 5, we should point out here that a halo of party unity hung over the Charter Conference. The major leaders at Kansas City so insisted on the appearance of party unity that many observers concluded that the basic conflict between old and new elements in the party was a thing of the past. And if support for the conference as a whole is a good indicator, then Kansas City was as successful as has been advertised. Eighty-four percent of the delegates sampled in our post-convention questionnaire responded to a query on how much the Charter Conference had helped or hurt the party (on a scale of $+3$ to -3) with either a $+2$ or $+3$. And what is equally important, those who preferred McGovern in 1972 were just as supportive of the outcome as delegates who had supported one of the "regular" candidates in 1972—Humphrey, Muskie, or Jackson.

The Evolution of Cleavages from 1972 to 1974: Some Evidence

Our discussion of this evidence will center on (a) the extent to which delegate goals in 1974 fit a model whose underlying dimension was a conflict between purist reformers and professional regulars, (b) the distribution of purist styles among McGovernites and regulars in 1972 and 1974, (c) differences in attitudinal support for the party among McGovernites and regulars, (d) a factor analysis of delegate attitudes in 1972 and 1974, and (e) a consideration of the contribution of purism-professionalism to the maintenance of cleavages.

Delegate Goals at Kansas City

In our pre-conference questionnaires, as well as in our interviews at Kansas City, we asked each delegate what he or she hoped to achieve at Kansas City. Many of the answers did fit what one might expect a regular to say, given the nature of the conflict in the party. For example, shortly before the midterm conference, the chairman of the South Carolina party, Don Fowler, who had just recently been elected national chairman of the Democratic State Chairmen's Association, remarked,

> Why are we writing a charter? Because the 1972 convention said we were going to write one. To my mind, the Democratic Party has thrived for 175 years without a charter, and I can't understand why we need one now.[12]

Of course, he may have feared that the document would serve to strengthen *national* party structures vis-a-vis state institutions, or that the new rules would reduce the flexibility of party leaders. Or he may have feared that the cost of a new charter would be a debilitating party disunity. But after the Kansas City meetings, Fowler expressed general satisfaction because "the Charter had not really changed very much."

Other delegates came with a broad overarching commitment to political change far beyond anything attempted by the 1972 reforms. Congressman Donald Fraser, national chairman of ADA (Americans for Democratic Action) and the original architect of the idea of a party charter, and political scientist James MacGregor Burns were "complete reformers." Just prior to the conference, Burns published his thoughts on the relationship between the business of the Kansas City conference and a reversal of the historical decline in party structures:

> So the real issue at the mini-convention will not be between regulars and reformers, nor between liberals and conservatives nor between blacks and whites. It will be between those who believe in party organization in the best old-fashioned sense and those who don't care if the parties die because they will be happy in a nonparty politics of powerful personal campaign organizations.[13]

But as it turned out, the attention of most delegates was focused on specific charter provisions rather than on broad organizational issues. They were concerned with current party practices and with marginal improvements in their own position within the party. While most accepted the creation of a charter as valuable, they conceived it as more a codification of present practices than an instrument for a thorough party reorganization.

The delegates' concern with incremental change was the product of two principal factors. First, delegates were to be presented with a fait accompli, a draft charter carefully constructed by the Charter Commission to assure its legitimacy. For the purpose of decision making at the convention, the document represented a status quo, departure from which could not be taken lightly.[14] Because the draft charter was a "party document," national party chairman Strauss was successful in his attempt to surround the document with symbols of party unity and loyalty, thereby picking up the support of delegates with no particular axe to grind and loyal to the party. Support for the draft charter became, in a symbolic sense, a way for the delegate to express his party loyalty. Thus, in the language of the convention, support for the draft charter became a code phrase for party unity. This can be seen quite clearly in the responses to our pre-convention questionnaires.

When the delegates were asked in the pre-convention questionnaire what was the most important result the charter conference could produce, the delegates split between party unity (44 percent) and a correct charter (44 percent). Twelve percent talked about a specific charter plank. The 44 percent of the delegates concerned with party unity were those who had come to the convention to support the draft charter.[15]

A second factor causing the delegates' incremental orientation toward change was the complexity of the draft charter. The draft contained a set of detailed interrelated provisions difficult to challenge in a convention setting. Groups dissatisfied with the draft charter realized early that attention would have to be focused in the pre-convention period on one or two major points. The Black and Women's Caucuses chose the affirmative action provision, as did the Meany-Barkan forces.

The effects of this pre-convention focus can be seen in the results of our questionnaire. When delegates were asked which issues would be important, 55 percent chose affirmative action. The next most popular issue was proportional representation. (It is clear from the questionnaires that a large number of delegates had confused proportional representation with affirmative action.) The charter provisions on centralization of the party evoked very little interest from most delegates. The convergence of expectations on the affirmative action provision had made it the big issue of the convention and a measure of how far the party would depart from the reforms of 1972. Thus the draft charter provision became a status quo, and a baseline for measuring change.[16] This development served to confine conflict at the convention to a well-defined issue on which groups had taken positions and communicated their stands to their followers. As a consequence, conflict was moderated in a way that could lead to its resolution at Kansas City. It is true, of course, that the so-called quota provisions had played a major role in the conflict at Miami and its aftermath. Thus, those who had been active in 1968 and 1972 could be expected to line up on the issue as they had on similar issues in 1968 and 1972.

Purist Styles Among 1972 McGovern Supporters and Regular Candidate Supporters

One of the major propositions in our 1972 analysis concerned the distinctions in political style we have come to label purist and professional. We had thought that such styles would be less in evidence (1) because Kansas City would be more a gathering of those involved in party affairs and less likely to attract ideologues, and (2) because of the moderating effects of two more years of party involvement on the part of McGovern supporters. The simplest test of our notion would be to examine changes in levels of purism represented at the 1972 and 1974 conventions; but the nature of the two conventions necessitated our choosing measures of purist orientation appropriate to each.

We have discussed our 1972 measure (see p. 23). In 1974 we used a simpler measure of purism-professionalism. Each delegate was asked on the pre-conference questionnaire:

"If you *had* to choose, which is most important? (*Circle one*)

Writing a correct charter
Making sure the party stays together

Those who put a unified party before a correct charter were called "professionals" and those who would seek a correct charter even though it might disrupt the party were labeled "purists." Because our measures of purism-professionalism differed in 1972 and 1974 it will not do to examine changes in levels of purism; a more useful strategy is to compare the extent to which purist and professional styles still differentiate McGovern supporters and the supporters of the "regular" candidates—Humphrey, Jackson, and Muskie. To accomplish this, we asked the Kansas City delegates, "Just prior to the 1972 convention, who was your first choice for a presidential candidate?" The question became, therefore, whether our measure of purism-professionalism based upon the political context of the 1974 convention distinguished delegate supporters of different candidates.

The evidence on changes in purism is mixed but generally supports the conclusion that substantial differences still remain. In 1972 McGovern supporters were 38 percent more purist than regulars (83 percent to 45 percent); the margin in 1974 was down to 31 perent, with the McGovernites at 70 percent and the regulars at 39 percent. Although the reduction was significant statistically, there remained a substantial gap in political style.

Despite the persistence of differences in political style in 1974, there is evidence that party office holding had some effect. If we look at those 1974 delegates who supported McGovern in 1972, we see that the most professional of the McGovernites were those who held party office prior to 1968 (43 percent). But for those who assumed party office a bit later—between 1968 and 1972—the proportion with a professional style drops to 31 percent. And finally, among those McGovernites who assumed party office after 1972, the proportion of professionals is lowest (16 percent). This finding can be interpreted as supporting the notion that party office holding, a reasonably good indicator of organizational activity and commitment, does have a moderating effect on purism; it shows, as we have argued, that one's political style is in part a consequence of one's organizational position. Yet party office holding has not reduced the overall level of purism significantly, because so many of the new activists have so recently entered the party (since 1972).

Party Support Among 1972 McGovern Supporters and Regular Candidate Supporters

Additional evidence for the persistence of old cleavages comes from an examination of attitudes toward party among McGovernites and the supporters of "regular" candidates. In both 1972 and 1974 we asked our delegates to rate the Democratic Party on a scale of

Table 3.3 Rating of Democratic Party by McGovernites and regulars, 1972–1974*

	McGOVERN SUPPORTERS IN 1972	SUPPORTERS OF HUMPHREY, JACKSON, OR MUSKIE IN 1972	DIFFERENCE
1972	+1.70	+2.37	−.67
1974	+1.44	+2.34	−.90

*The entries are average or mean ratings. Each delegate was presented the symbol "Democratic Party" and responded to it with an evaluation of +3 to −3.

+3 to −3. Table 3.3 reports average support scores for our delegate sample at the 1972 convention and for 1974 delegates who told us they had supported either McGovern or a "regular" candidate prior to the 1972 convention.

Two conclusions may be drawn from an examination of Table 3.3. First, the average level of support for the Democratic Party was far weaker among McGovernites than among regulars in both 1972 and 1974. Second, there was little change from 1972 to 1974. If anything, the differences in support were more pronounced in 1974 than in 1972.

Cleavages in the Party: A Factor Analysis of Attitudes toward Groups and Leaders, 1972–1974

The fourth body of evidence to be considered comes from a factor analysis of cleavages in 1972 and 1974. We have shown thus far in our examination of the evidence on political style and support for the party that classifying delegates by their 1972 candidate affiliation divides them into purists and professionals as well as into strong and not-strong party supporters.

In this section we shall take a slightly different approach. We shall first examine the attitudes of delegates in 1972 to see what evidence there is for the interpretation of the struggle there as limited to amateur purists vs. professional regulars. If the conflict was indeed limited to such a confrontation, we shall find that a Stage I model, assuming a single continuum on which all delegates can be located, will be most accurate. If on the other hand the conflict in 1972 was more complex, the Stage I model will turn out to be inadequate.

The most appropriate data we have for answering such questions come from our interviews with delegates at Miami and Kansas City. We asked each delegate to rate major figures and groups on a scale of +3 to −3. Our initial goal was to see how attitudes toward different political figures and groups went together. To achieve this we correlated, for our 1972 sample, each of the ratings with every other rating; we did the same for the 1974 sample.

The Meaning of a Correlation Coefficient. A correlation coefficient (in this case the product moment correlation) is a measure of how closely two attitudes go together.[17] For each attitudinal measure (Kennedy, McGovern, and so on), the average (or mean) for the delegates was found. Then each delegate was scored on how far he departed from the average for each measure. For example, a delegate may have been two units, or steps, above the mean in his affection for McGovern. A correlation coefficient indicates how accurately a delegate's departure from the average (or mean) on one measure (say support for McGovern) indicates his distance from the average (or mean) on a second measure (say support for the Black Caucus). If the distances on both measures are in the same direction (either above or below the mean), the correlation is positive in sign; if in opposite direction, it is negative.

A correlation between two measures (say support for McGovern and for the Black Caucus) is perfect if each delegate is exactly the same distance from the average score on support for McGovern as he is on support for the Black Caucus; if the distances are in the same direction, the value of the correlation coefficient is +1; if in the opposite direction, −1. But few correlations have values close to +1 or −1; they more often hover in the range of ±.50. A correlation of .50 means that a delegate one unit, or step, above the average on one measure is likely to be .5, or 1/2 that distance, above the average on the second measure. And a correlation close to 0 means that a delegate's distance from the average on one measure gives no indication of his distance from the average on the second.

For the 1972 and 1974 delegate samples we correlated delegate attitudes toward McGovern, Black Caucus, Women's Caucus, Ted Kennedy, Democratic Party, labor, Humphrey, and Wallace. Table 3.4 displays the correlations. The upper right triangle contains the

Table 3.4 Correlations between attitudes of delegates toward major figures and groups, Miami in 1972 and Kansas City in 1974*

	McGovern	Black Caucus	Women's Caucus	Ted Kennedy	Democratic Party	Labor	Humphrey	Wallace
McGovern		.51	.34	.49	.08	−.16	−.24	−.58
Black Caucus	.44		.49	.30	.12	−.02	−.09	−.41
Women's Caucus	.46	.60		.19	.10	−.07	−.05	−.22
Ted Kennedy	.42	.41	.32		.17	.10	.07	−.37
Democratic Party	−.02	.03	−.05	.12		.32	.40	−.03
Labor	−.14	.00	−.04	.15	.41		.28	.06
Humphrey	.11	.14	.03	.46	.32	.22		.10
Wallace	−.23	−.02	−.05	−.12	.12	.16	.08	

1974

1972

*Entries are product moment correlation coefficients based on +3 and −3 ratings of each concept by each delegate in the 1972 sample at Miami and in the 1974 sample at Kansas City.

1972 results and the lower left those for 1974. For example, look at the correlation between the attitudes toward McGovern and the Black Caucus in 1972 (.51, the first entry in the top row, second column). The +.51 means that attitudes toward McGovern and the Black Caucus went together—that those who liked McGovern also liked the Black Caucus and those who disliked McGovern also disliked the Black Caucus. Shift now to the correlation between attitudes toward McGovern and Wallace (−.58, the first row, last column). The minus sign indicates that those who liked Wallace disliked McGovern and those who liked McGovern disliked Wallace.

To find out how a person or group fared in 1972, start with the column in Table 3.4 bearing the desired name, for example, Kennedy. The correlations of attitude toward Kennedy with attitudes toward the concepts listed to the left of his column are given in the column (.49 with McGovern, .30 with Black Caucus, and .19 with Women's Caucus). For correlations of attitude toward Kennedy with attitudes toward those concepts listed to the right of Kennedy (Democratic Party, labor, Humphrey, and Wallace), find the *row* labeled "Kennedy" and read across starting on the right side of the main diagonal (.17 with Democratic Party, .10 with labor, .07 with Humphrey, and −.37 with Wallace). To discover the correlation for two attitudes in 1974, perform the analogous operations upon the lower left triangle in Table 3.4.

Does the Stage I Model Describe 1972 or 1974? Now we are in a position to examine the pattern of correlation to see what light it sheds on the notion of a single continuum, with which we began our investigation. The Stage I hypothesis of a single continuum suggests a correlation matrix with one great organizing principle—the location of the delegate on the regular-reform dimension. Thus the more reformist a delegate, the greater his affection for reform groups and leaders (McGovern, Black Caucus, Women's Caucus) and the greater his hostility toward regular groups and leaders (Humphrey, labor, the Democratic Party). These concepts would be joined in the reformer's mind because of his feeling that the regulars owned the party and that the reformers had been denied their due by the party. And a similar logic would work in reverse for the regulars; as their affection increased for regular groups and leaders (Humphrey, labor, and "their party"), their dislike of reformers would increase.

The Stage I model suggests, then, positive correlations between attitudes toward reform objects (those who like one like all and those who dislike one dislike all) and powerful negative correlations between each *reform* group leader and each *regular* group leader.

A cursory inspection of Table 3.4 reveals that the Stage I model is an inadequate organizing principle for 1972. To help the reader follow our explanation we have labeled selected groups of correlation coefficients in Table 3.4. First, examine the two A clusters. Attitudes toward reform groups and leaders went together as the Stage I model predicted, but their enemies were not the regulars (Humphrey, labor, or the party). The strong negative correlations supporting such an interpretation are simply not there. Rather, the attitude that most clearly indicates an anti-reform stance concerns George Wallace ($-.58$ correlation with McGovern, $-.41$ with the Black Caucus, and a $-.22$ with the Women's Caucus.)

Yet a distinctive regular dimension does emerge. Examine the items in cluster C (labor and the Democratic Party). One's attitude toward any one regular group or leader did indicate the strength and direction of one's attitude toward others (Humphrey, labor, and the party), although it said nothing about one's disposition toward reformers. Contrary to the assumption of a single continuum (the Stage I model), we need two factors or organizing principles to interpret properly the pattern of correlations for 1972; these are a reform/anti-reform and a regular/anti-regular dimension.

And the results for 1974, displayed in the bottom left triangle of Table 3.4, force us to the same conclusion. Cluster B represents the reform and cluster D the regular dimension. The similarity of the results to 1972 is striking. Yet, there is evidence of some subtle shifting in attitudes. The moderate negative correlation between attitudes toward Humphrey and McGovern in 1972 ($-.27$) became mildly positive in 1974 ($+.11$); thus Humphrey no longer stood opposed to a major reform leader. Second, the attitude toward Kennedy in 1974 was correlated positively with attitudes toward McGovern ($+.42$) and Humphrey ($+.46$); in 1972 Kennedy was identified almost exclusively with reform groups and leaders. Finally, the profound isolation of Wallace in 1972 lessened considerably by 1974 (compare his column with his row in Table 3.4).

To show the cleavage structure in 1972 and 1974 with more precision, we have subjected the correlation coefficients in Table 3.4 to a factor analysis—a technique that puts into mathematical form what we have already described in terms of clusters in the

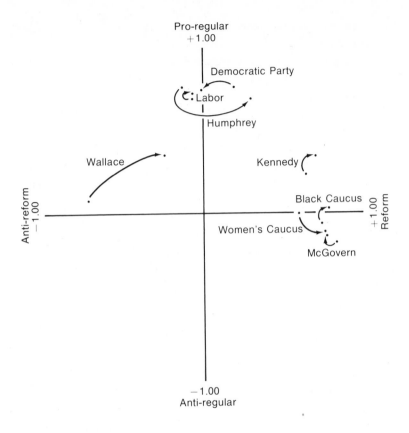

Figure 3.2
Factor structure of 1972 and 1974 Democratic Party delegates. Each concept is placed in the two-dimensional space according to its loading, or correlation, with each factor. The points plotted are 1972 loadings; the arrows indicate their movement to the 1974 positions.

	1972		1974	
	Regular	Reform	Regular	Reform
McGovern	−.171	.832	−.137	.772
Black Caucus	−.060	.741	.029	.783
Women's Caucus	−.003	.597	−.113	.759
Kennedy	.236	.640	.347	.701
Democratic Party	.764	.192	.750	−.009
Labor	.695	−.067	.730	−.067
Humphrey	.763	−.135	.659	.294
Wallace	.084	−.725	.354	−.245

table. The results are shown graphically in Figure 3.2.[18] The two axes, which are at right angles to each other, represent the two basic organizing principles for understanding the pattern of correlations. The location of each concept on a factor represents its correlation with that factor. Like any correlation coefficient, it can range from $+1$ to -1 in value. The two factors in Figure 3.2 are easily identifiable as the same reform and regular factors we isolated in our description of the clusters in Table 3.4. The points plotted are 1972 correlations with the two factors; the arrows indicate their movement to 1974 locations.

Evolving Party Cleavages: Interpreting Factor-Analytic Results.
We have spoken of two attitudinal factors—a regular and a reform dimension—that account for most of the variation in attitudes at the convention. In terms of Figure 3.2, we can think of organizational loyalty or attitudinal support for the Democratic Party as varying from $+1$ to -1. The high positive scores for Humphrey and labor on the regular factor mean (1) those who disliked Humphrey also disliked labor, (2) those who liked Humphrey also liked labor, and (3) the explanation for (1) and (2) may be found in what Humphrey and labor shared—*a close identification with the Democratic Party.* And similarly, the high positive scores on the reform factor for McGovern and the Black Caucus suggest that (1) those who liked McGovern also liked the Black Caucus, (2) those who disliked the Black Caucus also disliked McGovern, and (3) the congruence in attitudes toward McGovern and the Black Caucus can be explained by their being identified as important components of the reform movement within the Democratic Party.

Now let us examine the relationship between the reform and regular factors. The reform axis in Figure 3.2 is perpendicular to the regular axis, indicating that movement along one of the axes says nothing about movement along the other. Note that McGovern and the Black Caucus have high scores on the reform factor but almost zero scores on the regular factor. Conversely, labor and Humphrey have high scores on the regular factor but low scores on the reform factor. In factor-analytic terms, such a result is called a simple structure. It means (1) that knowing a delegate's score on the regular factor says nothing about his attitude toward reformers and, conversely, (2) that the score on the reform factor provides no information on how the delegate feels about the party establishment.

Figure 3.2 puts in a more striking and graphic form what we have discovered in interpreting the pattern of correlations in Table 3.4. The notion that a Stage I model would describe the configuration of attitudes in 1972 was clearly mistaken; there is no single continuum along which to array delegates that constitutes an adequate explanation of the Table 3.4 correlations. As our factor analysis demonstrates, two dimensions—reform and regular—are required. The two-dimensional nature of the conflict in 1972 may be the concluding phase of an earlier change begun in 1968, or it may simply evidence the erroneous views most of us held of the complexities of the 1968–1972 period. Unfortunately, we do not have the evidence at hand to resolve the issue.

The analysis for 1972, and subsequently for 1974, does clarify what has been a puzzling aspect of the cleavage structure in the party—the relationship between Wallace, the reformers, and the regulars. Figure 3.2 shows quite strikingly that the reformers and Wallaceites stood at different positions along the same dimension, and that attitudes toward them were independent of their attitudes toward regulars. The reform/anti-reform dimension was in 1972 occupied at one end by McGovern and the caucus groups, and at the other by Wallace. Attitudes toward the regular groups and leaders—Humphrey, labor, and the party—varied quite independently of their feelings toward Wallace and the leaders of reform groups. And as the factor analysis shows, labor, Humphrey, and the party clustered tightly around the axis representing the regular dimension.

If we now turn our attention to the shift in pattern since 1972, what first strikes the eye is the rather substantial movement of Wallace toward a stronger position on the regular dimension and a much less polarized one on the reform dimension. In addition, Humphrey moved from a slightly anti- to a slightly pro-reform position. And Kennedy continued to drift in the direction of higher correlations with both the reform and the regular factor; this suggests that as a delegate became either more reformist or regular, his affection for Kennedy grew.

But the most striking feature in the comparison of 1972 and 1974 is the relative stability of the two factors—reform and regular—as devices for describing the cleavage structure. The same faces and groups reproduced in 1974 the cleavage structure of 1972.[19] Yet there were new issues, groups, and persons active in the deliberations at Kansas City. What effect did they have on the cleavage structure?

Most of the significant new faces at Kansas City belonged to the new candidates for the party nomination in 1976. We know the decison to put the charter into effect in 1980, thus excluding the short-run nominating politics of 1976, would lessen the impact of candidate organizations, and thus the delegates' candidate preferences, on conference deliberations. Moreover, the new candidates tried as much as possible to avoid taking positions on the issues, leaders, and groups that had split the party in 1972.

To gain some measure of impact, we factor analyzed the correlations between our measures of attitude toward each of seventeen concepts.[20] To the eight concepts discussed we added nine others, for a total of seventeen. Thus in Figure 3.3 we show results for six active or potential candidates (Wallace, Kennedy, Bentsen, Udall, Bayh, Jackson), four reform groups or persons (McGovern, Women's Caucus, Black Caucus, Democratic Planning Group), and seven traditional groups or persons (DNC, state delegation, labor caucus, Coalition for the Democratic Majority, the Democratic Party, Humphrey, Strauss). Because of the importance of the Charter Commission's work, we included its chairman, Terry Sanford.

Three factors were extracted accounting for almost 50 percent of the total variance. The largest factor was the regular factor, with high loadings on DNC, labor caucus, state delegation, the Democratic Party, Bentsen, Strauss, Jackson, and Humphrey. For the second largest factor, candidate dimension, the persons with the highest loadings were Udall, Bayh, McGovern, anti-Wallace, and Kennedy. The third factor was a reform factor; the highest loadings were for the Women's Caucus, the Black Caucus, anti–Coalition for a Democratic Majority, Sanford, and McGovern. The first and third factors are the reform and regular (Figure 3.3) dimensions we have already explored.

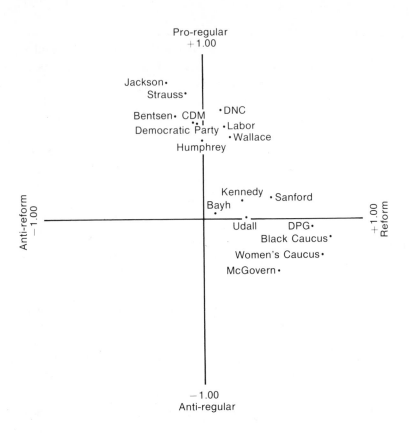

Figure 3.3
Full cleavage structure at Kansas City, 1974. Each concept is placed in the two-dimensional space according to its loading, or correlation, with each factor.

	Regular	Reform		Regular	Reform
Jackson	.828	−.229	Wallace	.495	.166
Strauss	.766	−.112	Bayh	.038	.071
Democratic			Sanford	.134	.420
Party	.583	−.041	Udall	.013	.262
Bentsen	.623	−.177	DPG	−.042	.680
DNC	.659	.110	Black		
Kennedy	.113	.240	Caucus	−.107	.798
CDM	.587	−.062	Women's		
Labor	.559	.131	Caucus	−.216	.741
Humphrey	.476	−.009	McGovern	−.314	.464

The emergence of an independent candidate factor testifies to the successful insulation of the conference from nomination politics as well as to the impact of fresh faces. Note in Figure 3.3 that three of the new candidates—Sanford, Bayh, and Udall—occupy positions near the center of the two factors. Whether a delegate was regular or reformer had little to do with his attitude toward any of the three candidates. But, on the liberal-conservative candidate factor (which is not graphed) there were sharp differences between candidates. In this sense, then, new candidates could take issue positions without arousing old antagonisms. In general, attitudes toward old candidates correlate most strongly with attitudes toward old issues and groups, with one exception—Kennedy. As we have shown, he was well regarded by both reformers and regulars. And yet he compares favorably with Udall and Bayh on the liberal side of the candidate factor. But note that the locations of Jackson, Humphrey, Wallace, and McGovern in Figure 3.3 are consistent with old regular-reform battle lines. Wallace's location does not seem intuitively correct until one realizes (see Figure 3.2) that he is much more on the reform/anti-reform dimension than on the regular dimension. And we have already documented his migration in 1974 to a less extreme position on the same dimension.

The above analysis contains some hints on the evolution of cleavages. First, the fact that the cleavage structure in 1972 and 1974 was at least two dimensional offers some promise for creative political leadership. The potential effect of a Kennedy candidacy has been consistently appealing because he has been able, by a combination of political style and issue position, to attract support from both reformers and regulars. (Note the shift of Kennedy in Figure 3.2.) As long as the cleavage structure stays complex, the possibility of bridging conflicts exists. Second, old cleavages are tied to old candidates and groups. Our discussion of Figure 3.3 suggests that as new candidates take the field, old cleavages will seem less relevant. Finally, issues change. The Kansas City conference dealt with issues left over from 1972, which brought back memories of old battles over group quotas and their political significance. But societies have a way of making old conflicts obsolete by moving on to new issues.

Of course, it is possible that the above conditions will not materialize, and that the conflict between reformers and regulars will re-emerge in a simpler form. Coalition building, especially in intra-party politics, where the party label is absent, forms around candidates whose personalities come to symbolize issues. The revival of presidential candidacies that arouse old antagonisms may well reproduce old cleavages. And if the issues in 1976 come to turn on the status of blacks and women in the party and in society, old wounds may be reopened.

Thus far in our exploration of cleavages in the period 1972–1974, we have probed with tools very sensitive to any evidence of multidimensionality. When answering our attitude questions, the delegates were not forced to choose between competing priorities as they might in the heat of battle. Thus they could express, if they so chose, affection both for regular and for reform groups. Yet, the differences between regulars and reformers emerged because in 1968 they were compelled to choose between issue purity and party loyalty. The battle between reformers and loyalists might better be thought of in terms of the different priorities each attaches to organizational survival and issues. The reformers put issues first; the loyalists, organizations.

Because the attitude measures on which we based our factor analysis did not force the delegate to choose between competing priorities, we shall now shift our focus to a measure that does—a version of the purism-professionalism variable modified to include an indicator of basic attitudinal support for the party.

Purism-Professionalism and Cleavages in 1974

In this section we shall show, using a procedure informed by but different from factor analysis, that the reform-regular conflict involved three distinct groups at Kansas City: (1) caucus groups concerned with social representation for women and minorities, (2) party professionals concerned with party unity and the maintenance of their own positions in the party, and (3) national party reformers who hoped to build institutional foundations for a strongly centralized Democratic Party. As it turns out, groups (1) and (3) were somewhat purist in the primacy of their concern with issues, while groups

(2) and (3) were professional in the sense that they had a strong loyalty to party.

From our theoretical perspective, we thought a useful measure of purism vs. professionalism would include (*a*) a simple indicator of identification or affection for the party and (*b*) a comparison of how important a correct issue position is in relation to party unity. Because most of the delegates (88 percent) were strong party identifiers, we used a slightly more sensitive measure. In our interviews at Kansas City, we asked each delegate to rate his affection for the party on a scale of $+3$ to -3. Forty-four percent of the delegates gave the party the highest possible rating, and in Table 3.5 this group is shown as having strong affection for the party; those who rated the party anywhere from -3 to $+2$ are labeled "not strong."

To measure the primacy of organizational loyalty, in the pre-convention questionnaire we asked each delegate, "If you had to choose, which is more important: writing a correct charter or making sure the party stays together?" Combining the answers to these two questions gave us a four-fold classification of delegates and a more sensitive measure of purism vs. professionalism (Table 3.5).

First, there were the party loyalists (35 percent) whose affection for the party is strong and who value party unity above issues — the classic professional. Second, there were the issue-oriented delegates (38 percent), willing to sacrifice — if need be — party unity to a correct charter (although it should be mentioned that some saw

Table 3.5 The distribution of political styles at Kansas City, 1974

	AFFECTION FOR THE PARTY		
	NOT STRONG	STRONG	
ISSUES MORE IMPORTANT THAN PARTY UNITY	Purists 38%	Centralizers 9%	47%
PARTY UNITY MORE IMPORTANT THAN ISSUES	Moderates 18%	Professionals 35%	53%
	56%	44%	100%(145)

a correct charter as one that would unify the party). The third group, the centralizers (9 percent), saw the party as a unique forum for the articulation of issues and mobilization of support for them. They saw a strong party organization and emphasis on issues as mutually reinforcing. This group, although tiny, did play a role at Kansas City. The final group—the moderates in Table 3.5—consisted of those who had no great affection for the party and yet considered party unity more important than issues. They were midway between the purists and the professionals; they shared with the professionals an interest in party unity and with the purists a less than perfect affection for the party.

In the statistical analysis that follows, we shall deal with the 91 percent of the delegates who fall on the dimension ranging from a purist style (issues important, weak affection for party) through a moderate (party unity important, less than perfect affection) to a professional style (strong affection for party, party unity of prime importance). The centralizers, the 9 percent who combine elements of both purist and professional styles, are excluded from the analysis; they will receive extended attention later.

From our earlier work in *The Politics of Representation,* we knew that the strong party person who valued party unity would fit most closely the mold of the standard professional concerned with problems back home and devoted to winning elections in his own constituency. National issues—and this includes charter issues—would be interpreted in terms of their effect on local party affairs. To measure variations in this national-local orientation, we examined the interview records of each of the 145 delegates interviewed at the convention for signs of a national or local focus. Wherever the delegate talked about charter issues in terms of local arenas and problems, we scored the sentence -1; where the delegate spoke in national terms and about national arenas, we coded the sentence $+1$. The national-local variable is simply the sum of the local and national scores. We used a simple correlational technique to assess how closely localism was associated with professionalism. If all professionals were local and all purists were national in orientation, the correlation would be perfect, or $+1$. If, conversely, all professionals were national and purists local, the correlation would be -1.

The particular measure we used in the following analysis is called Gamma. Our theoretical expectations, using the national-localism index, were borne out handsomely: the Gamma between our measure of party professionalism and the national-local index was a whopping $+.60$, indicating that those who professed a strong concern for party unity tended to worry most about their local arena.

Because the classic professionals were so strongly local in their orientation we had hypothesized their reluctance to go along with the more centralizing provisions of the draft charter. Using attitude toward the Judicial Council as a measure, we see some confirmation of the hypothesis in that the more professional the delegate orientation, the stronger the opposition to the Judicial Council (Gamma $= .23$).

Our model led us to believe as well that the locally-oriented professional (more concerned with party unity than issues) would strongly oppose the nationally-oriented minorities' (blacks' and women's) attempt to secure on a national level what they felt was denied them on the local and state level—equal access to power in local and state parties. Thus we thought that the Black and Women's Caucuses would be liked the least by the party professional. Our expectation was borne out quite handsomely; the more professional the delegate's orientation the less favorable his attitude toward either the Black or the Women's Caucus (Gamma $= -.47$ and $-.45$ respectively). To complete the picture we had hypothesized that the traditional arm of labor—COPE—would be liked most by the locally oriented professional. And that was indeed the case (Gamma $= +.49$).

Our results with the index of purism-professionalism are evidence of a simpler cleavage structure. By *forcing* the delegates to choose between competing priorities, we have deliberately fused the reform and regular dimensions which our earlier factor analysis so carefully separated. The fusion can be seen clearly in a factor analysis in which we added the "party unity or correct charter" variable to the eight attitudes (McGovern, Black Caucus, Women's Caucus, Kennedy, Democratic Party, Humphrey, labor, and Wallace) analyzed earlier. The results suggest that purism-professionalism had a high correlation with both the reform and regular factors; a purist response expresses an anti-regular and pro-reform sentiment while a professional response is pro-regular and anti-reform. Clearly then, we could force delegates at Kansas City to respond as if they were purists or professionals. Yet the drama of the conference was arranged so that delegates would not have to choose between party unity and issue purity (a correct charter). Although relevant, such choices were not as salient as they had been in 1968 (when many McCarthyites bolted the party) or in 1972 (when many regulars had to come to grips with such a choice).

Reformers, Regulars, and Centralizers: The Bargaining Context at Kansas City

Most of those at Kansas City—reformer as well as dedicated party professional—considered themselves strong Democrats. The reformers had a vision of a more nationally oriented party, which would further guarantee their access to decision-making power in the party. Their goals were very instrumental. They wanted strong national institutions to force more adequate representation of certain social groups in state and local party affairs. For example, party rules adopted at the national level require that state parties undertake programs of affirmative action with reference to *state* party bodies (for example, state committees). In the case of state delegations to national conventions, if these plans are not implemented to the satisfaction of a national compliance review commission, there are provisions for national intervention in state party affairs. Thus, for those delegates, centralization was to be a means of guaranteeing social and interest representation through institutions like the Judicial Council, the Education and Training Council, and the programs of affirmative action, which would function as analogues to the landmark federal civil rights legislation of the 1960s. On the other hand, the classic professional, committed to his local base of power and worried about winning, wanted to avoid issues that would fragment the party. Thus he could be loyal to the same party but have a different vision of its composition and organization.

Somewhat paradoxically then, delegates to the 1974 conference who placed a premium upon party identification and loyalty were often those favoring decentralization. Proponents of strong national institutions for promoting greater social representation also argued that citizens should be able to flow into (and out of) party processes and positions whenever mobilized either by highly salient issues (for example, the Vietnam War) or by a felt need for greater social representation. They did not, therefore, view a binding party identification as an end in itself to be achieved by strong national structures, as delegates like James MacGregor Burns and Donald Fraser did. Rather, they thought new groups would pledge loyalty to the party in exchange for increased representation. In fact, those placing primary emphasis upon social representation (Article X) were perceived as weakly enough identified with party to make a walkout threat credible. And their threat to bolt the party struck centrally at the desire of the professionals to hold the party together for 1976.

The affirmative action compromise that climaxed the conference was achieved through accommodation between those who had come to Kansas City with the primary goal of achieving strong provisions for social representation (the Women's Caucus and the Black Caucus) and those most desirous of keeping the party together, the professionals (Robert Strauss, Richard Daley, Don Fowler, the governors).

But what of the other group of reformers—the 9 percent who wanted to create strong national party institutions in order to better articulate issues? Some of the reforms in this category (mandatory midterm conferences, four-year terms for national party chairmen, and authority for the national party to establish criteria for participation in party affairs) were defeated. Others (Judicial Council) were passed in a compromise form. But the "national party" reforms never captured the attention of the delegates in the same way that affirmative action measures did.

Why didn't the centralizers fare better at the conference? The answer, simply stated, is that there were too few of them, and their tactical position at the conference was weak. In order to achieve their goals, those (like Burns and Fraser) favoring a strong national party would have had to convince the locally oriented professionals (like Fowler) that strong national structures would rejuvenate the party and, as a consequence, enhance the prospects for electoral victory. But the reformers themselves were split between those who were interested in a strong national party as an important goal in itself and those who saw national party institutions as a vehicle for group goals. Because a substantial part of the reform coalition seemed so willing to give up party identification when it did not serve their interests, many regulars had serious qualms about any moves to strengthen national institutions.

In any event, the conflict over these institutions, although an important one to party theoreticians, never got to the center of the conference stage; there, professionals were fighting out the issue of social representation with the Black and Women's Caucuses. (The 1972 version of the charter drafted by Fraser even called for a system of national party membership. This was strongly opposed by blacks in the period just prior to the 1972 convention.)

In conclusion, then, we feel that it is a bit misleading to view the Kansas City convention as limited to a conflict between reformers and the party establishment. There was, as we have shown, a cleavage within the reform group, stemming from competing priorities among charter provisions. This division was more severe than might otherwise have been the case, because a key bargaining counter that was used to secure the goals of those seeking social representation worked against acceptance of the arguments raised by those desiring party centralization. The threat of a walkout by blacks and women was an effective one, given the desire of professionals for a unified base in 1976. That threat did call into question the legitimacy of the group caucuses in the eyes of some of the more traditional party delegates, and it certainly did not increase these delegates' enthusiasm for yielding power to new national institutions that might be dominated by the group caucuses. The fact that the Black and Women's Caucuses could command such attention at the conference represented a remarkable change from 1972; in the next chapter we shall focus directly on the experience of those groups.

Notes

1. The question of the name given the conference held in Kansas City in December 1974 is indicative of the dispute that arose surrounding this unprecedented institution. The original title contained in the 1972 resolution was "Conference on Democratic Party Organization and Policy," indicating the intention of its namers to discuss both charter questions and substantive issues of public policy. Liberals began referring to the 1974 meeting as the "Policy Conference," while those who fought hard in the Democratic National Committee to confine the meeting to charter matters used the term "Charter Conference"; many actors opted for the neutral label "Midterm Conference."

2. See, for example, F. J. Sorauf, *Party Politics in America* (Boston: Little, Brown, 1972), Chapters 5 and 9; or T. W. Madron and C. P. Chelf, *Political Parties in the United States* (Boston: Holbrook, 1974), Chapter 4.

3. D. G. Sullivan et al., *The Politics of Representation* (New York: St. Martin's, 1974), Chapter 5.

4. See pages 72–76 and 84–86.

5. Actually, no credentials challenges alleged discrimination solely on the basis of delegation composition; charges of procedural violations accompanied evidence in the form of social composition. In addition, few of the challenges were sustained, yet the effect of these rules was to stimulate an unprecedented number of challenges.

6. The wording approved by the Democratic governors during their November meeting in Hilton Head (N.C.), and borrowed from the language of the Mikulski Commission, reads as follows with deletions and italicized insertions finally adopted at Kansas City:

    > Performance under an approved Affirmative Action Plan and composition of the convention delegation shall be considered relevant evidence in the challenge *of any State delegation.* If a State Party has adopted and implemented an approved *and monitored* Affirmative Action Program, the Party shall not be subject to challenge based solely on delegation composition or *solely on* primary results.

7. See, for example, an analysis of charter issues by J. M. Burns, "Kansas City Scenario," *The Washington Post,* December 5, 1974.

8. D. G. Sullivan et al., *The Politics of Representation,* Chapter 5.

9. S. M. Lipset, *Political Man* (New York: Doubleday, 1960).

10. D. G. Sullivan et al., *The Politics of Representation,* Chapter 5.

11. Ibid.

12. Personal interview at Kansas City.

13. James MacGregor Burns, "Kansas City Scenario," *Washington Post,* December 5, 1974.

14. If we were to develop a nominating convention analogue to Kansas City, the Charter Commission draft would be the major candidate with a strong

majority coming into Kansas City and Strauss would be the campaign manager. The leaders of the respective caucus groups, and possibly the coalitional group leaders, would be analogous to minority candidates hunting for bargaining counters to pry concessions from Strauss.

15. As we walked around the convention floor during the proceedings we noted a number of delegates thumbing industriously through a large book put out by the DNC explaining each charter provision, while a speaker at the podium droned on about some provision. There was little bargaining or decision making of any sort; it was a desultory show. We asked some of the delegates to the convention where the major decisions were being made. They replied with gusto, "Right on the convention floor, of course." Most of the delegates replying in this way had come committed to the draft charter.

16. This seemed to us a major achievement of the pre-convention period and a tribute both to Strauss and to the work of the Charter Commission. It made possible an orderly convention as well as an orderly conflict. Strauss and the DNC managed to create a situation in which the establishment occupied a position between the Democratic conservatives and liberals, an ideal position for performing a brokerage function.

17. The discussion of correlation assumes equal standard deviations or the transformation of the variable into standard score form.

18. A principal-components factor analysis with a varimax rotation was used. The 1972 analysis extracted two factors explaining 63 percent of the common variance. The 1974 analysis added a candidate factor to the reform and establishment factor, explaining again about 60 percent of the common variance. The similarity of the results is surprising given the slightly different measurements made in the two cases. In 1974 we used a scale of $+3$ and -3, but in 1972 we used a thermometer ranging from zero to one hundred degrees, with fifty degrees representing indifference. To make the scales comparable, we collapsed the thermometer scale so that it had seven categories. The data analysis was done under Project IMPRESS routines at Dartmouth College.

19. The results were sufficiently surprising that we went back and examined mean attitude scores for each of the maor concepts in 1972 and 1974. There is no evidence that on the average the attitudes toward the reform groups have gotten more positive or, for that matter, that members of the reform groups have gotten more positive about the regulars.

20. See note 18 for our procedure.

The Institutionalization of Group Caucuses

4 CHAPTER

Demands for Direct Group Representation, 1968–1972

In 1968 the Democratic Party was in the throes of adjusting to the demands of groups with newly won positions of power in American politics. Although the party thought of itself as representing those who demanded change in society, spokesmen for the groups most concerned with change did not agree. From the perspective of many blacks in America, the Democratic Party was basically white. For activist women, the party was overwhelmingly male. And for young people just becoming involved in politics, the party was in the hands of the old. The leaders of these newly active groups declared that the middle-aged, white, male regulars who exercised decisive control in the party would never understand or accept their needs and aspirations.

For some, then, the party needed reform, and reform could only move in one direction. Distrust of the regulars by leaders of new power groupings led to a demand for direct representation in the policy-making procedures of the party.

Traditionally, group demands have been filtered through the party apparatus on local, state, and national levels. Representation has been indirect, the responsibility of those who have made politics a life-long commitment and who see themselves as professionals. The demand for direct representation was thus a challenge to the legitimacy of an old profession.

Furthermore, the form of direct representation proposed for the 1972 convention—caucuses of blacks, women, and youth— raised a challenge to the classic model of convention decision making. According to that model, bargaining at a convention is carried out among state delegation leaders and candidate organizations. But in the weeks preceding the 1972 convention, group caucus leaders and outside observers were predicting that group caucuses would become the central arenas for decision making at the convention.

The Miami Beach convention may be seen as an experiment in direct group representation. For various reasons to be discussed shortly, the group caucuses did not become the force at the convention that some had hoped or expected. In 1974, however, direct representation of functional interests—blacks and women—became more of a reality; it was hailed as a success by delegates to the Charter Conference and by journalists who wrote about the conference. By comparing the 1972 and 1974 experiences, we can learn something about the contending groups within the Democratic Party, the institutionalization of groups, and patterns of decision making at conventions.

High Hopes and Organizational Problems, 1972

The experience of the caucuses in 1972 did not justify their organizers' optimism or the observers' expectations. Although there were meetings during convention week of a Black Caucus, a Women's Caucus, and a Youth Caucus (as well as a Latin Caucus, a

Senior Citizens' Caucus, and a Jewish Caucus), none of these groups was able to become a major decision-making force at the convention; most could not even make a sustained claim on the attention of their potential members. A number of caucus leaders had hoped to draw up lists of issue positions and then bargain with candidates to secure their support for the positions, but this never occurred.

Given these difficulties, it is not surprising that the 1972 delegates were not impressed by the power of the caucuses. Our research, based on interviews with a random sample of delegates, showed that at the outset of the convention, no group caucus was thought by more than 30 percent of the delegates to be a site of the most important convention decisions; as convention week progressed, delegates decreased their estimates of the potency of group caucuses.[1]

The failure of the group caucuses to meet expectations in 1972 can be explained by a number of recurring organizational problems. One of these was the problem of time. Because of the fast pace and heavy workload of the convention itself, delegates were often in a rush, and they could not afford the time to go to special caucus meetings. Caucus leaders and participants found that there was not enough time to carry out the ambitious strategies that some of them had planned.

Another organizational problem for the caucuses was self definition; it proved difficult for these groups to set and maintain their own boundaries. Who, for example, should be allowed into a black caucus? That caucus tried to restrict its membership to delegates and alternates but found it impossible to keep non-delegates out. Finally, the decision was made to let any black person into the meetings of the Black Caucus, with full voting privileges. But this decision created other problems; it was hard for people to hold delegates to a decision in which numerous non-delegates had participated.

A final and crucial problem for the special caucuses was that other organizations—notably candidate organizations—felt their own goals might be threatened by the existence of strong, independent group caucuses. The McGovern organization, for example, had serious reservations about an active youth caucus, and McGovern aides tried to discourage the senator's young delegates from building an independent youth group. There were also some clashes between the McGovern organization and the Women's Caucus over a strong abortion plank and other issues. For delegates with multiple group identities, there were internal strains. Those who had a stake in the nomination of a particular candidate proved to be unwilling to drop their commitment to that candidate in favor of loyalty to a group caucus. McGovern delegates, many of whom had played a leading role in the development of the caucuses, were willing to subordinate caucus loyalty to candidate success.

The importance of the candidate organizations at the 1972 convention was widely acknowledged by the delegates. Among decision-making arenas at the convention, the McGovern organization was perceived by delegates to be the most important. Over 50 percent of the delegates viewed the McGovern organization as the site of the most important decisions at the outset of the convention, and that figure rose to over 70 percent by the end of convention week.[2]

Although the group caucuses might have attained some importance as sites at which candidate organizations could communicate with delegates, the candidates' aides in fact listed delegates by state and contacted them through state delegations. For a number of reasons, state caucuses proved to be popular places for meeting and communicating. Delegates had to attend these caucuses to receive their floor credentials and guest passes for the gallery—items of considerable importance. Members of state delegations were housed together in Miami Beach; they had been selected at common conventions or in the primaries back home; and the delegates had often known each other prior to the national convention. In addition, state delegates would have continuing political relationships with each other in the future.

Because of these organizational factors, the special group caucuses were no match for the candidate-organization/state-delegation combination as communication units for decision making at the 1972 convention. Although the caucuses seemed clearly to have fallen short of their initial goals, the perception of failure was far more pronounced among non-members than among members. In fact, over the course of the convention there developed in each case—women, blacks, and youth—a rather peculiar phenomenon

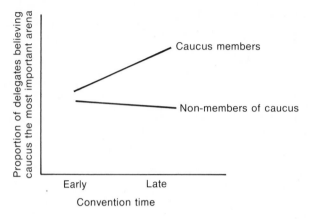

Figure 4.1
Typical divergence of perceptions of the importance of caucuses during the 1972 Democratic presidential nominating convention.

in which the perception of one's own group as an important decisional arena increased while the non-member's perception went in the opposite direction. In *The Politics of Representation* we cited this as evidence of the growing insulation of the caucus movement. Figure 4.1 diagrams the process. For example, early in convention week blacks and whites were pretty much agreed on the importance of the Black Caucus as an important arena (30 and 28 percent respectively). By Friday, however, the proportion of blacks calling their caucus the most important arena had doubled while the proportion of whites agreeing had dropped from 28 to 5 percent. In *The Politics of Representation* we argued that the candidate organizations rendered the caucuses impotent and that their institutionalization in a convention setting would have to await a time when candidate organizations were non-existent, impotent, or deadlocked in a classically brokered convention. We thought that the Kansas City convention would offer a good test case; the conditions for caucus effectiveness appeared to be present.

As in 1972, we developed a questionnaire instrument that enabled us to assess changes in delegates' perceptions of important decisional arenas. Because a short three-day convention offered neither observer nor participant sufficient time to do much observing or participating, we examined the perceived importance of

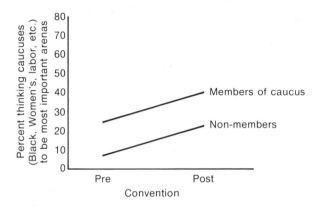

Figure 4.2
Changes in perception of caucus importance among caucus members and non-members.

The wording of the question was: "Where do you expect the most important decisions at the conference to be made?" A list of arenas followed and the delegate was asked to circle one name. A caucus member was a delegate who described his role at Kansas City as a member of one of the caucus groups.

arenas by comparing answers to pre-convention and post-convention questionnaires. Although the samples overlap considerably, we have presented our results in Figure 4.2 for the entire pre-convention and post-convention sample. Figure 4.2 does not show the convergence predicted by our model, but it does indicate that the perception of caucus importance at Kansas City grew equally among caucus members and non-members. As befitted a convention in which caucus groups were remarkably effective, there was a growing belief in their importance.

Group Caucus Success, 1974

From the beginning of the conference the caucus groups concentrated their attention on Article X, Section 6 of the proposed party charter—which spelled out the guidelines for challenging delegations on grounds of inadequate affirmative action. In November of 1974, the Democratic governors, meeting at Hilton Head, South

Carolina, had voted to support the affirmative action rules adopted by the party's Mikulski reform commission.[3] But leaders of the Black and Women's Caucuses felt that these rules, which placed the burden of proof on challengers, would make affirmative action challenges extremely difficult to sustain. They pointed out that such challenges at the 1974 meeting had not been successful, and that the percentages of women and blacks on state delegations had decreased from the 1972 convention to the 1974 conference. At Miami Beach in 1972, 36 percent of the delegates were women and 14 percent were black; at Kansas City in 1974, 33 percent were women and 9 percent were black.[4]

At the 1974 conference, the Black and Women's Caucuses persuaded a number of other important actors—first some liberal union leaders, then Democratic governors, then party chairman Robert Strauss, and finally a majority of the delegates—to support them in altering Article X, Section 6 to make affirmative action challenges easier to sustain. In their analyses of the convention, journalists credited the Black and Women's Caucuses with a significant victory:

> The women, the blacks and Latinos, all came out winners in the mini-convention. They demonstrated their cohesion and organizational talents, and required liberal party leaders—who in the past often had bypassed them—to enlist their cooperation.[5]
>
> The problem was that blacks and women felt that they had been left out of the supposedly final compromise on participation in party affairs. It was not so much that they objected to the substance of the compromise.
> As one black leader remarked late last night, "I think it's what you people call a power play."
> After hours of pressure and threats, the blacks and women succeeded in moving the centrist pragmatists (Mr. Strauss and the Governors). So they won, they won because they saw that they had the power, and they succeeded in bringing it to bear.[6]
>
> The big deal was struck by the women and the blacks on the one hand, and the Democratic governors on the other.[7]

Thus group caucuses were recognized as having exerted substantial influence on the outcome of the 1974 party conference—a far cry from their role in 1972. What were the reasons for the change? To answer this question, we must look at changes both in the outside environment and within the caucuses themselves.

External Factors

Perhaps the most crucial difference in the external environment of the group caucuses in 1974, as opposed to 1972, was the absence of active candidate organizations to compete with the caucuses for delegates' time and loyalty. Presidential candidates, both announced and unannounced, were at the Kansas City meeting—Scoop Jackson handing out Washington apples, Lloyd Bentsen throwing large receptions, George Wallace holding press conferences, Morris Udall distributing issue statements, Jimmy Carter meeting delegates, and so on—but candidate organizations did not take an active role in the struggles over the charter. Thus, as our factor analysis in Chapter 3 showed, group caucus members did not experience conflicts between their roles as candidate supporters and their roles as caucus participants.

The caucuses were also aided by a convention schedule that was more relaxed than the hectic pace of 1972. And this was related to the absence of a presidential nomination. Delegates did not feel the same sense of urgency about an issues panel that they would have felt about a credentials vote or even a platform debate. Thus there was more time to attend group caucus meetings.

Another environmental factor that aided the Black and Women's Caucuses was the split among the labor delegates at the convention. Although AFL-CIO President George Meany and his chief political aide, Al Barkan (director of the Committee on Political Education), had been the chief antagonists of the Black and Women's Caucuses in party struggles over group quotas and affirmative action, it soon became clear at Kansas City that Meany and Barkan did not speak for all of labor. Indeed, liberal unions— American Federation of State, County and Municipal Employees, Communication Workers of America, United Auto Workers, and Machinists—offered crucial support to the demands of women and minorities. Therefore it became difficult for a "labor caucus" to act as a unified and effective group.

The proposition that labor could not act as a unified force gains further support when we look at the attitudes of those who were favorable toward COPE and those who were favorable toward the labor movement. In our post-convention questionnaire we asked

Table 4.1 Correlations between attitudes of delegates in 1974 toward labor and toward caucus groups and the affirmative action compromise*

	LABOR MOVEMENT	COPE
Affirmative action compromise	+.30	−.43
Black Caucus	.01	−.49
Women's Caucus	.01	−.58

*Entries are Yule's Q coefficients for the variables dichotomized as equally as possible.

delegates to rate COPE and the labor movement on a 7-point scale, ranging from −3 to +3, as well as a number of other issues and groups. We then correlated ratings of COPE and the labor movement with attitudes toward the affirmative action compromise, the Black Caucus, and the Women's Caucus. The results are presented in Table 4.1. Each entry is the correlation coefficient between attitude toward the concept in that column (either labor movement or COPE) and row (either the affirmative action compromise, the Black Caucus, or the Women's Caucus). Table 4.1 shows clearly that those who felt favorable toward the labor movement supported the affirmative action compromise while those favorable to COPE were far less supportive. In addition, we see that delegates liking COPE were far less supportive of the Black and Women's Caucuses while attitudes toward the labor movement were independent of attitudes toward the caucus groups.

The pattern of correlation in Table 4.1 provides rather striking evidence of a divergence between those who were favorable to labor as a whole and COPE supporters. The "events" of the convention were the strength of the group caucuses and the affirmative action compromise. Willingness to support the compromise became a true measure of one's commitment to party unity. And it is in the compromise that supporters of the labor movement and COPE disagree most strongly (a difference of .73 in the value of the correlation).

Finally, the Democratic governors at the conference, by agreeing to work for changes in the language of Article X, Section 6, provided legitimacy to the position of women and minorities. The governors, who had received considerable acclaim for their Hilton Head attempt to unify the party, became a focal point of delegate and observer attention at Kansas City. At first, the governors were reluctant to change the wording of their previous compromise draft. But persuasion from women and minorities (including the threat of a walkout by black delegates), together with intercession by some liberal union leaders, changed the governors' minds.

Internal Caucus Institutionalization

Besides being helped by certain external factors, the Black and Women's Caucuses were also aided in achieving their objectives by the internal institutionalization they were able to develop. N. W. Polsby has stated that

> for a political system to be viable, for it to succeed in performing tasks of authoritative resource allocation, problem solving, conflict settlement, and so on, in behalf of a population of any substantial size, it must be institutionalized. That is to say, organizations must be created and sustained that are specialized to political activity. Otherwise, the political system is likely to be unstable, weak, and incapable of servicing the demands or protecting the interests of its constituent groups.[8]

Two of the characteristics ascribed by Polsby to an institutionalized organization are the following:

> 1) [Such an organization] is relatively well-bounded, that is to say, differentiated from its environment. Its members are easily identifiable, it is relatively difficult to become a member, and its leaders are recruited principally from within the organization. (2) The organization is relatively complex, that is, its functions are internally separated on some regular and explicit basis, its parts are not wholly interchangeable, and for at least some important purposes, its parts are interdependent. There is a division of labor in which roles are specified, and there are widely shared expectations about the performance of roles.[9]

One important difference between the group caucus experiences in 1972 and 1974 was that in 1974 the caucuses were better able to define their membership, to set boundaries between themselves and the outside environment. In 1972, the Black Caucus had argued about who was eligible for membership in it. The group found it difficult to limit its membership, and all black people who wanted to participate were allowed to do so. But in 1974, observers were carefully separated from the delegates and alternates in the meeting room. At the first caucus meeting, a rope was placed across the back of the room and observers were directed to sit behind it. Only delegates and alternates were allowed access to the two microphones, which were placed in the front of the room. Thus the Black Caucus had drawn a very visible boundary between itself and the outside world. And that boundary was made even stronger at the second caucus meeting, to which only delegates and alternates were allowed admission. (Because of the delegates' concerns about the problems of openness and accountability that were posed by this approach, eight black journalists were also admitted to the meeting.[10])

A second difference between the caucuses in 1972 and 1974 was the increased internal complexity and organization that could be observed at Kansas City. In 1972, both the Black and Women's Caucuses were largely forums for hearing presidential candidates and speeches by their own members. Neither group had developed a communication system for the convention floor or a stable leadership structure. But in 1974, both caucuses had much more sophisticated operations. The Women's Caucus divided the convention floor into five general areas; each of these "quadrants" comprised certain state delegations. Each delegation had a Women's Caucus floor leader, who was expected to be in frequent communication with her quadrant leader. Two women acted as overall floor coordinators. The Black Caucus also established a communication system, with eight floor leaders assigned to various areas of the convention hall. The floor leaders were to relay instructions to the delegates, and Earl Craig (chairman of the Democratic National Committee's Black Caucus) acted as a courier between floor leaders.

An important indicator of institutionalization is the development by an organization of a specialized leadership function. In both the Black and Women's Caucuses at Kansas City, small groups of prominent delegates were selected to serve as steering committees. The Black Caucus' steering committee included California Assemblyman Willie Brown (who served as chairman), U.S. Representatives Yvonne Braithwaite Burke and Charles Rangel, and DNC Vice Chairman Basil Patterson. Members of the Women's Caucus steering committee included Representative Bella Abzug,

Barbara Mikulski, who had headed the party's reform commission, and Patt Derian, a national committeewoman from Mississippi.

After having observed the relatively formless and chaotic group caucus meetings at the 1972 convention, we were struck by the degree to which caucus leaders in 1974 were able to hold the attention of caucus members and to direct their energies. From the beginning, leaders in both the Black and the Women's Caucus focused on Article X, Section 6 as the crucial item of business at the conference. Patt Derian began the first Women's Caucus meeting by discussing what she said was the one goal of women at the convention—the deletion of Article X, Section 6. Leaders of the Black Caucus also focused on that section in their first meeting, which ended with a vote for deletion. (The group caucuses later modified their goal—to *changing* Section 6—in the interests of attracting outside support.)

At no time during the four Black Caucus meetings or the three Women's Caucus meetings was there serious questioning of the leadership's identification of key issues, group positions, or strategies. Single delegates might rise from time to time to suggest other issues or to complain that proposed compromises were "sellouts," but there were no sustained challenges. Votes were carried by acclamation. Armed with this support, the leaders were able to convince their respective caucuses to act in strategic ways to maximize their influence at the conference. When some delegates at the second Black Caucus meeting wanted to strike a charter provision that appeared to give certain special advantages to women, caucus leaders persuaded the delegates that such an action would endanger the coalition they were trying to build with women. At the same meeting, chairman Willie Brown refused to permit a vote on any motion for a walkout. It was sufficient for negotiating purposes, he explained, to have the caucus record that such a motion had been put forward. Similarly in the Women's Caucus, leaders frequently talked about the value of gaining "half a loaf" as a step in the preferred direction.

The ability of caucus leaders to unite their groups around realizable goals enabled them to appear moderate enough to gain outside support, but there were times when the leaders encouraged their caucuses to take a harder line as a move in the negotiating process. When party chairman Strauss proved resistant to calls for the deletion of Section 6, California Congressman Ron Dellums and Los Angeles Mayor Tom Bradley sponsored a strong resolution in the Black Caucus. That resolution said that the deletion of Article X, Section 6 had become an issue of principle to the Black Caucus, and that the caucus was prepared to walk out if the deletion were not accomplished. The motion was supported by established black leaders like Representative Rangel and Detroit's Mayor Coleman Young, and it carried unanimously. This vote enabled the leaders to use Schelling's "commitment" strategy in negotiations.[11] Having committed one's reputation to holding firm on a particular point, concession is made much less likely. Thus in a variety of ways the caucuses' internal cohesion and willingness to accept leaders' recommendations gave those leaders certain advantages as negotiators.

In interviews conducted by our researchers at group caucus meetings, delegates often spoke proudly of their group's organizational performance at the conference:

> [The Women's Caucus will be] the strongest single force in the convention. It's well organized, has the most attendance . . .
> —Women's Caucus member

> We've had an educational focus, and the caucus has been a good one.
> —Black Caucus member

> It's incredibly well organized. Everyone is accepting the compromise. Each state's women's political caucus is really well organized.
> —Women's Caucus member

In all, the differences in the experience of the group caucuses in 1972 and 1974 were considerable.

State Delegations

As in 1972, state delegations served as important information and communication centers for delegates. Over 80 percent of the delegates in our sample identified state delegations as "most helpful" in "keeping in touch with conference developments." Besides performing housekeeping functions—like informing delegates about the next day's agenda—state delegation meetings were forums for group caucus representatives to communicate their position to other delegates.

Other Groups

There were some groups who tried to become umbrella organizations for delegates having similar ideological views and attitudes toward reform. But these groups—the Coalition for a Democratic Majority (relatively conservative Democrats) and the Democratic Planning Group (relatively liberal Democrats)—were not very visible at the conference. Unlike the Women's and Black Caucuses, who focused their energy on a single issue, these other groups scattered their efforts among a wide range of party issues. As one member of the Democratic Planning Group said of this organization: "I can't tell truly how effective we are. . . . We're certainly a force, but it's not clear toward what end we are using that force." The fact that affirmative action and Article X, Section 6 became the central issue at Kansas City may be attributable to the well-defined focus and organizational strength of the Black and Women's Caucuses, compared to other groups at the conference. Thus our pre- and post-conference interviews give ample testimony to the decline in perceived power of the coalitional groups; 59 percent of our pre-convention sample thought CDM or DPG to be most powerful while in the post-convention sample only 39 percent did. A good part of the decline is due to the sharp drop in the perceived power of CDM (the tactical arm of labor and Jackson at the convention) from 22 percent in the pre-convention period to 10 percent afterwards.

Impact on Others: The Problem of Legitimacy

Although the members of the Black and Women's Caucuses had reason to feel satisfied with the outcome of the conference, we might expect other delegates to express concern or resentment about one of the means by which they won—the threat of a black walkout. What implications did this have for the way in which the delegates viewed the conference and the legitimacy of its decisions? Did the conference make Democrats more or less conciliatory toward each other? It is to these questions that we now turn.

Notes

1. For amplification of this point and presentation of data, see D. G. Sullivan, J. L. Pressman, B. I. Page, and J. Lyons, *The Politics of Representation: The Democratic Convention, 1972* (New York: St. Martin's, 1974), pp. 45–58. Also see J. L. Pressman and D. G. Sullivan, "Convention Reform and Conventional Wisdom: An Empirical Assessment," *Political Science Quarterly,* 89 (Fall 1974), pp. 550–551.

2. See Sullivan et al., pp. 64–65.

3. See "Democratic Governors Uphold Compromise on the Make-Up of the Conventions," *New York Times,* November 19, 1974.

4. For the 1972 figures, see Sullivan et al., p. 23.

5. J. Witcover and A. Scott, "'Unity' Hailed by Strauss," *Washington Post,* December 9, 1974.

6. R. W. Apple, Jr., "Recasting McGovern Reforms," *New York Times,* December 9, 1974.

7. D. Nyhan, "Democrats: New Party Scenario, No Star," *Boston Globe,* December 9, 1974.

8. N. W. Polsby, "The Institutionalization of the U.S. House of Representatives," *American Political Science Review,* vol. 62, March 1968, pp. 144–168.

9. Ibid., p. 145.

10. Among those admitted was Andrea Wolfman, a Smith College student and one of our interviewers. We are grateful to Ms. Wolfman for her observation of Black Caucus meetings, and to K. Reimann, a Dartmouth student, who observed the Women's Caucus.

11. See T. C. Schelling, *The Strategy of Conflict* (New York: Oxford University Press, 1960).

CHAPTER 5

The Problem of Legitimation

Conventions, like other social organizations, move through what Talcott Parsons has called phases.[1] First, there is problem definition and information acquisition. Second, there is the task to be achieved, which for the Kansas City convention was the voting of the charter provisions. Finally, there is the solidarity phase, in which the tensions and conflicts of the task period are dissipated and contending groups attempt to re-establish their common commitment to the organization.

In presidential nominating conventions, the solidarity phase following the nomination is expressed as a call for party unity and a commitment on the part of both winners and losers to the electoral task ahead. Indeed, one of the more celebrated functions of party nominating conventions is their legitimation of the presidential nominee as a candidate that all segments of the party can support. (Legitimation may be said to occur if the various components of the party believe that the procedures and decisions of the convention were fair and proper, and that, as a consequence, the final result should be supported.)

Political scientists have often commented upon the unifying and legitimating functions of conventions. For example, V. O. Key declared that:

> The convention provides a means for the contending candidates, factions, and interests within a party to consult and agree upon the terms on which they will work together in the presidential campaign. The resulting concert of interests exerts a formidable power throughout the nation.[2]

Yet when the Republican Party met in San Francisco in 1964 to nominate Barry Goldwater, liberal Republicans (Rockefeller, Romney, and Scranton) refused to support the party's nominee. And in 1968 many McCarthyite delegates repudiated Hubert Humphrey as the nominee of the Democratic Party. In a similar fashion, many Democratic regulars left Miami in July of 1972 unwilling to work for George McGovern. From 1960 to 1972, of the six conventions with non-incumbents competing for the nomination at convention time, three were clearly nonlegitimating. Conventions, then, are not automatically unifying occasions; and their results are not necessarily perceived as legitimate by all segments of the party. Because the successful performance of the legitimation function cannot simply be taken for granted, we must look more closely at the preconditions of legitimation and the ways in which various groups of delegates come to terms with the results of a convention.

In this chapter we shall first discuss how the distinctive institutional characteristics of charter and nominating conventions facilitate or inhibit the process of legitimation. In general, we shall conclude that in the modern period conventions of the charter type have more potential than nominating conventions for producing outcomes perceived as fair or legitimate. Our comparative analysis will be followed by the presentation of some data from our Kansas City study bearing upon some theoretical notions concerning legitimation. Finally, we shall conclude the chapter by arguing that a charter convention's distinctive advantage in legitimation may stem from its resemblance to the classic model of convention decision making.

The first condition discussed in *The Politics of Representation* concerned the need for the winning coalition to take into consideration the interests of the losing coalition. In exchange for such consideration, the losers pledge themselves to support the winner. If the exchange is successful, it is called party unity, and a presumably unified party can then turn to the task of winning the general election. If the issues dividing winners and losers are of such magnitude that they make each potential compromise seem a betrayal of the vital interests of either party, such an exchange will not take place.

Presidential nominating conventions have special difficulties in satisfying this precondition. The time for bargaining and compromise is short, and the stakes are large and not very divisible. The presidency is indeed a big prize, and it is easy to upset emotionally those denied a chance to obtain it. In nominating conventions winners and losers are clearly defined, making it difficult for the losers to imagine themselves—in some sense—winners.

Party charter conventions, on the other hand, may resemble legislative bodies more than they do nominating conventions, and thus offer more opportunities for delegates to see themselves as winners. Instead of one big prize—the nomination for president—there are a number of charter provisions. Thus it is possible for a delegate losing on one provision to win on another. And it is easier for a delegate to see himself a winner because charter provisions are often ambiguous in their language and consequences. Aware of this ambiguity, enterprising leaders can come together to arrange compromises so that each can convince his followers that they have won on the essential points, or that the word changes in the compromise provision are trivial. This, in fact, was the rumor circulating on the 1974 convention floor concerning the governors' compromise proposal on the affirmative action provision.

The Divisible Prizes at Kansas City

Although there were twelve prizes, in the form of draft charter provisions, the focus of attention was Article X, Section 6. As a head of steam built up over Article X, the other provisions were debated and voted in an atmosphere described quite nicely by one delegate:

> Meanwhile, we were also passing the charter, article by article, with sometimes sharp but always decorous debate. Voice vote and roll call. There should be no mandatory policy conferences (one for the right). There would be a judicial council to put party affairs under the rule of law (one for the left). The majority ruled. The minority accepted.[3]

A minor theme was the conflict between the centralizers (left) and the professionals (right). There would be no formal rules for membership in the party; the judicial council would exist but not be powerful; the idea of a truly national meeting to make national policy on which candidates would run was scotched, although the possibility of future meetings was left open. There were not many centralizers on the Charter Commission or on the delegations, so the charter was far from what most wanted; yet it did provide some symbolic reward for their efforts.

The major confrontation, to which we now turn, involved party professionals and the Black and Women's Caucuses negotiating Article X, Section 6. The governors, at their Hilton Head, South Carolina, meeting proposed that the Charter Conference adopt the Mikulski Commission's rule covering the 1976 presidential election in which Section 6 read,

> Performance under an approved Affirmative Action Plan and composition of the convention delegation shall be considered relevant evidence in the challenge of any State delegation, *but composition alone shall not constitute prima facie evidence of discrimination, nor shall it shift the burden of proof to the challenged party.* If a State Party has adopted and implemented an approved and monitored Affirmative Action Program, the Party shall not be subject to challenge based solely on delegation composition or solely on primary results.[4] [Underlined words not in the original.]

Black and Women's Caucus leaders were appalled by the governors' proposal and argued for its deletion, claiming its presence would make challenges too difficult; the deletion would shift the burden of proof to the challenged party. Conservative labor leaders said that without the provision, Article X would reinstate quotas; they threatened to walk out if Section 6 was deleted. The governors, now at Kansas City, again came to the rescue, working out a compromise with leaders of the Black and Women's Caucuses, which involved the deletion of the italicized words above and the insertion of the eight underlined words. Some conservative labor leaders thought they had lost; others were not so sure. Black Caucus leaders claimed victory. Mayor Hatcher was quoted by columnist David Broder as saying, "I think it is a substantive change. We have stronger language now than in 1972."[5] The governors assured members of their own state delegations that the change was nothing much. Ann Wexler of Connecticut was reported as saying, ". . . this doesn't mean quotas; it really means affirmative action."[6]

The substantive consequences of the compromise on Section 6 were quite unclear, thus allowing those wanting a favorable outcome to find one and, of course, permitting those left out—such as conservative labor leaders—to claim that their vital interests had been sacrificed for the compromise. The compromise, then, was something of a Rorschach ink blot—an ambiguous stimulus interpreted by partisans according to their deepest wishes.

Yet the prizes were on the whole a unifying factor. The Charter Commission had created an acceptable draft, and the amendments gave symbolic satisfaction to both left and right. Moreover, the eventual affirmative action compromise facilitated the work of partisans on both sides.

To sum up, a convention of the charter type more easily satisfies the first precondition because (1) the very notion of winning and losing is ambiguous, (2) a charter consists of many planks, which can be used to build support in different groups in the party, and (3) the consequences attached to any particular plank are subject to a variety of interpretations. It is hard for either side in such a situation to argue that "giving in" would betray its vital interests.

The second precondition discussed in *The Politics of Representation* concerns the prospect for winning the general election. The energy that fuels the process of mutual adjustment and eventual legitimation is the prospect of winning office. When it is poor, the incentive for party unity is weak. Even when the prospects are good for a successful challenge to an incumbent, there is not always agreement on which candidate might best capitalize on the opportunity. It is widely accepted among scholars of the subject that when voters step into their voting booths, their perception of the incumbent's past record is of prime importance in determining the out party's chances. The out party can do little to alter this. If the incumbent has been an utter disaster, almost any challenger nominated by the out party will win; if he has been an immense success, the out party can do little more than accede gracefully to another four-year term for the incumbent. But the political situation of the incumbent is sometimes more ambiguous. It can be divisive if (a) the party activists think the incumbent can be beaten and (b) they differ sharply on which candidate is capable of doing it. Something like this seems to have happened in 1972 when the out party—the Democrats—saw the Republican incumbent as less than invincible. Yet there was sharp disagreement among party activists concerning McGovern's chances against Nixon; 72 percent of the McGovern delegates thought McGovern would win while 72 percent of the Muskie-Humphrey-Jackson delegates were just as sure McGovern would lose.[7] The disagreement over which candidate might best exploit Nixon's weaknesses was a further source of polarization in the party.

In 1974 the tactical position of the party had changed considerably since 1972; Watergate and the economy had induced a mild political euphoria in those assembled at Kansas City. Disasters such as inflation and unemployment seem to evoke in politicians the same mixture of sorrow and self-interest that the prospect of a plague does in morticians. The expectation that the party might reoccupy the White House in 1976, coupled with the absence of presidential nomination politics, acted to heighten the incentive value of party unity.

The final precondition for legitimation discussed in *The Politics of Representation* concerns the political style of those who conduct convention business. Effective politics requires a political style that we have labeled professional. In general, as we have shown earlier, a professional is by definition one who places a high value on party unity, while the purist tends to focus on the party as an instrument for the articulation of issues. Those who pursue purist aims in party politics are viewed as disruptive because they prevent the carrying through of "normal politics." Kansas City was a meeting of professionals, people active in party and elective politics.

Except for the brief flurry of caucus activity late Saturday afternoon, the political styles adopted by leaders were generally non-purist. Even Bella Abzug spoke of the value of compromise and party unity at the Saturday afternoon meeting of the Women's Caucus. At Miami in 1972 most delegates (64 percent) were purists; at Kansas City in 1974 they were mostly professionals (51 percent).

We have now completed our survey of the differences between nominating and charter conventions in their capacity for legitimation. They may be summarized as follows. First, the accommodation between winners and losers is facilitated at charter-type conventions because losers on one issue (provision) can become winners on another, and the ambiguity surrounding charter provisions may cloud the sense of who has won or lost on a particular issue. Second, the expectations concerning electoral victory are more likely to have a polarizing effect in a nominating, as opposed to a charter, convention. Third, charter conventions attract those more interested in and thus committed to party affairs. Their level of party attachment tends to be higher and compromise enjoys more respectability.

The Legitimation Process from the Point of View of the Delegates

Our analysis thus far may suggest to the careful reader that a convention satisfying the preconditions of legitimation will be a dull affair, a consequence, it might be argued, of the fact that a legitimate outcome is assured. The reader is partially correct. Conventions are indeed fragile institutions, which require an enormous amount of support if they are to survive. This is the reason for our rather strong statement of the pre- (or necessary) conditions for legitimation. A weak institution needs a nurturing environment. It cannot long sustain challenges by powerful and disgruntled losers. Yet the process by which winners and losers reach an accommodation at the convention site is not without dramatic and theoretical significance. It is, of course, much more complicated than a simple coming together of group leaders in a smoke-filled room or in back of the speaker's podium. Leaders must be able to speak for and commit their followers. And delegates must be able to follow leaders, and commit themselves on a psychological level. To understand this interaction between leaders and followers we must grasp the ways in which delegates think about themselves and their role in the decision-making process.

It is valuable to remember that politicians seek power for themselves *and* for groups they represent (or identify with). Of course, they want other things, but as they all learn, the acquisition of power is the key to getting the other things. If groups that a politician represents continually suffer power losses, the politician's reputation for power—and thus his power itself—suffer as well. A politician must improve the power position of groups he represents if he is to maintain his own. Most delegates are politicians and such reasoning is not foreign to them. Because delegates represent the party as well as other groups they want to see its power maintained and enhanced. And they conceive of its power on the national level in terms of the prospects of its nominee for occupying the Presidency; the Presidency and Vice-presidency are the only nationally elected offices. But winning an election means little to the delegate-politician if the groups that he represents have little claim on the newly elected president. Therefore, they are driven to evaluate convention outcomes (charter provisions or presidential nominees) in terms of gains and losses for the groups they represent.

The way in which the delegates calculate gains and losses is partly determined by the strength of their desire for party unity. When it is strong, delegates are motivated to search for ways to support the outcome. To maintain their self-esteem as effective politicians, delegates must find groups that they represent (or identify with) who are advantaged by the outcome. Of course, the advantage does not have to be real. If, as may have been the case at the charter convention, the outcome is ambiguous, delegates can more easily fashion supportive interpretations.

The raw material for such interpretations rarely includes knowledge drawn from direct participation in the decision-making process. Delegates in large collective settings—having no way to gauge precise gains and losses—can examine provisions and candidate statements, read about negotiations, or listen to those who purport to lead them. Using these cues they decide who was powerful in determining the outcome and, from that, who was advantaged or disadvantaged. When the political drama played out on center stage is ambiguous, such cues may be the only aids for delegates in their calculations.

In that case, delegate attributions of power to groups and their leaders may be of decisive importance in the legitimation process. If a power attribution is made to a group represented by a delegate, he may experience vicariously the joys of power exercised by the group's leaders. Because the politician's function is to advance the goals of groups he represents, an attribution of power to group leaders allows the delegate to feel that he has discharged his duty. Conversely, events sometimes make it impossible for the delegate to attribute power to "his" groups, so that he becomes a clear loser and, as a consequence, alienated from the decision-making process.

Analytically, then, the interesting question to be answered concerns the causes of power attributions. From the point of view of our theory, two principal factors stand out—the delegate's desire for party unity and his or her multiple group memberships. We have discussed the former; the latter can be stated quite simply. The larger the number of groups that the delegate represents, the more probable it is that he can discover a constituent group advantaged by a particular outcome. The drive for party unity acts as an incentive; the multiple groups of the delegate are alternative pathways toward an integrative solution, one consistent with the delegate's desire for party unity and the success of his constituent groups. The appearance, if not the reality, of power is necessary if the politician-delegate is to support the convention outcome. Politicians wish to preserve and enhance both their power and their reputation for power. It is important, then, that they locate pathways to consensus because they represent the solution of the problem of integrating their desire for party unity with their desire for the success of groups they represent. Of course, if party loyalty is low and a delegate lacks a complex set of identifications (or constituent groups), he will support the outcome only if it advances his particular group goals.

Because it is so important for delegates to discover constituent groups that are beneficiaries, those who arrange the drama of negotiations must take special care to provide the mass of delegates with appropriate group leaders. In the next section we shall turn to a description of the drama at Kansas City and a presentation of data concerning the legitimation process there.

The Psychological Function of the Confrontation at Kansas City

In this section we shall first describe the convention proceedings from our standpoint as observers. Then we shall consider a statistical analysis of the role of power attribution in the legitimation process at Kansas City. Both accounts strongly support the theoretical notions concerning the legitimation process that we have introduced in the preceding pages.

As we observed the unfolding of the convention, it seemed to us that the ambiguity of the affirmative action compromise, with the drama of the final negotiation, was of decisive importance. It allowed those who identified with the major participants to see themselves as "winning" or, in a minimal sense, "not losing." The confrontation was arranged so that most delegates could attribute power to groups or persons they identified with and, thus feel advantaged by the outcome.

For the caucus members, the task was easy. Those who most strongly identified with the caucus groups were most likely to accept the arguments of their leaders that something less than deletion of Section 6 was a victory. But there were women and some blacks who neither identified with the caucus nor shared its concern for affirmative action. These women could think of themselves as adherents of the regular groups or leaders participating in the compromise—the governors at the conference, Terry Sanford of the Charter Commission, the DNC, the Rules and Amendment Committee, the governors at Hilton Head, and Robert Strauss.

Because of this collage of groups most regular delegates could somehow identify with the winning side in the dispute, and thus interpret the outcome as favorable. For example, if a delegate came to Kansas City as a labor delegate committed to the Coalition for a Democratic Majority, he might see the Coalition and labor as having suffered a defeat. Yet he might identify with Strauss, the

DNC, and the governors—all of whom turned out to be powerful. Thus he could respond to their appeals for support and experience a sense of power and satisfaction as well. In the same way, women feeling that the Women's Caucus had gone too far could find groups on the other side with whom they identified and that were perceived as having brought about the compromise.

Turning now to our statistical analysis of levels of legitimation and changes in power attributions over the course of the convention, we shall see in more detail the way in which our theory of legitimation was confirmed. Our first step in the analysis was to examine the post-convention questionnaire rating ($+3$ to -3) of how much the conference helped or hurt the party. We used the rating as our basic measure of legitimation. The fact that 84 percent of the delegates at Kansas City answered with either $+2$ or $+3$ is impressive testimony to the solidarity-building function of the conference; the different shadings in support allowed us to identify those people who felt relatively more supportive of the conference. We divided our sample into two groups—those very favorable toward the conference outcome and those slightly less favorable— and correlated the conference rating with various measures of group membership (Table 5.1). For purposes of comparison, we

Table 5.1 Support for the conference as a whole and for the affirmative action compromise (AAC) by major groups active at the conference*

	Cope	Labor Delegate	Member of Women's Caucus†	Non-White	Party Professional
Conference	$-.30$	$+.15$	$.00$	$+.47$	$-.24$
AAC	$-.43$	$.00$	$+.39$	$+.77$	$+.06$

*All coefficients are either Gamma or Yule's Q, the equivalent for Gamma in the 2×2 case. Support for COPE is measured on a 7-point attitude scale; a COPE supporter was defined as one who scored above the median. A labor delegate was by definition one who indicated in the post-conference questionnaire that his labor role had been either first or second most important to him at Kansas City. An analogous definition was used for Women's Caucus members. Because of the few blacks in the post-convention sample, we took all our non-whites. A party professional was a delegate who valued party unity over a correct charter. Support for the affirmative action compromise was measured on a 7-point scale; the distribution was dichotomized above and below the median.

†Coefficient computed for women only.

have included correlations of the same group membership measures with support for the affirmative action compromise.

The correlations in Table 5.1 indicate, comparing group members and non-members (COPE, labor, Women's Caucus, minorities, party professionals), how much more likely a group member is to support (a + sign) or oppose (a − sign) either the charter or the affirmative action compromise. For example, the +.77 correlation in the bottom row of Table 5.1 indicates that non-whites (a minority) are far more likely than whites to show greater than average support for the affirmative action compromise.

We can gain some sense of the legitimating effect of the convention by comparing the bottom row of correlations in Table 5.1 (which indicate relative satisfaction with the affirmative action compromise) with the top row (indicating relative satisfaction with the conference as a whole). The two groups commonly believed to have benefited from the events at the conference were Women's Caucus members and non-whites. Indeed, as the correlations in the bottom row of Table 5.1 show, these two groups emerge most satisfied with the affirmative action compromise (+.39 and +.77 respectively); this means, looking at the other side of the coin, that non-caucus women and whites were relatively less satisfied.

The legitimation power of the conference for those who saw themselves losers in a relative sense can be measured by their willingness to join with the winners in support of the Charter Conference as a whole. The correlations in the top row of Table 5.1 give us some indication of this willingness. *The smaller the values of the correlations in the top row, the greater the agreement among factions on the value of the charter as a whole.*

Given the high level of support for the charter conference as a whole, the absence of disagreement among potential opponents on its value (as measured by a low or zero value in the top row of Table 5.1) can be taken as evidence of legitimation (of winners and losers uniting in their affirmation of support for the charter). Note that the coefficients for Women's Caucus members vs. female non-members (.00) and whites vs. non-whites (+.47) are much lower for support of the charter than of the affirmative action compromise. Although the legitimating effect was far more profound for women than for whites, it did take place for both groups.

Let us turn our attention to a conflict in which a particular group —labor—was perceived to have lost on the affirmative action provision. Yet those delegates considering themselves representatives of labor felt no less support for the compromise than other delegates (.00 in the bottom row of Table 5.1). And they were even more supportive of the conference as a whole (+.15 in the top row) than were non-labor delegates. But if we examine the attitude toward COPE —the political arm of the AFL-CIO active at Kansas City—we discover that those who liked COPE disliked the affirmative action compromise (−.43) and were only a little less displeased with the charter as a whole (−.30). As we shall argue later, this result suggests a cleavage between labor leaders and labor delegates at the conference. For those who thought of their principal role at Kansas City as representatives of labor, both the compromise and the Charter Conference as a whole were perceived as legitimate. This was not so for those who supported COPE.

For the last group, the professionals, the correlation in the bottom row of Table 5.1 indicates that they were no less satisfied with the compromise than others. But they are the one group whose relative satisfaction was lower for the Charter Conference (−.24) than for the compromise (+.06). This apparently stemmed from their dislike of the basic idea of holding a conference.

To explain how the changes in each of these groups fit, or fail to fit, our theory of legitimation, we shall treat successively the following: women, COPE, labor, and party professionals. We do not have a large enough sample for an adequate analysis of blacks. However, we shall include comparative material on blacks where it seems useful.

Groups and Legitimation: The Case of Women

Of the three caucus groups—women, labor, and blacks—the women present the most fascinating material for the application of our theory. A majority of blacks coming to the conference identified with the Black Caucus (60 percent) and were willing to use the threat of walkout to achieve their goals. Women, on the other hand, were far more divided both on identification with the Women's Caucus and on the desirability of using a walkout threat to achieve their goals; a little less than one-third of the women at the conference identified themselves as caucus members.

Women's Caucus members tended to be younger (twice as many were under 35 compared with non-members), were more issue-oriented (17 percent more likely than non-members to say a correct charter was more important than party unity), and were a bit less strongly identified with party.

The split between women caucus members and non-members may have been procedural as well as substantive. In our interviews with the women, it seemed clear that some non-members wished to pursue women's goals through regular Democratic channels whereas caucus members wished the party to acknowledge the power and, thus legitimate the role, of women in party affairs. Evidence for this interpretation comes from a variety of sources.

First, non-caucus women were less supportive than members, or even men, in their evaluation of the Women's Caucus. As a middle-aged woman pointed out in answering our question concerning the Women's Caucus, "I resent women expecting things just because they're women." This did not mean that she opposed affirmative action; she opposed the notion that there was a distinctive female interest deserving separate representation. At best, non-caucus women were somewhat uneasy with the notion of a women's caucus as an independent force in party affairs. In our post-convention questionnaire we asked the delegates to rate the Women's Caucus on a scale of $+3$ to -3; caucus women gave the caucus a rousing $+2.67$ rating while non-caucus women were slightly less favorable ($+0.52$) than men ($+0.58$). Second, non-caucus women disliked the affirmative action compromise involving the Women's and Black Caucuses more than caucus women, or males. Third, when the word "compromise" was removed from our questionnaire item and "charter provision on affirmative action" was substituted, non-caucus women became more positive in their evaluation. Finally, when we asked each delegate to rate how much the conference helped or hurt the party, there was no discernible difference in the reactions of caucus and non-caucus women (see Table 5.1).

There were in fact three women's factions. First, there were the women committed to affirmative action as defined by the Women's Caucus. A committed Women's Caucus delegate from the Midwest told us Friday night, twenty-four hours before the compromise settlement,

> The reason I came here was to promote women's rights. Any power or foot in the door or friends we can make is advantageous or worthwhile. I'm against the Governors' Compromise which puts the burden of proof in a credentials dispute on the accuser. That is against every piece of civil rights legislation which ever passed. The Women's Caucus has an amendment to delete that tomorrow.

Second, there were the women—already discussed—who accepted the goals of affirmative action but felt that regular party channels would be sufficient to achieve them. They rejected the need for a special women's interest group. Finally, there were women who rejected both the need for affirmative action and the Women's Caucus. A strongly Democratic middle-aged woman from the Midwest told us, "I want to retreat from the exclusionary McGovern reforms." And she expressed a dislike for the caucus groups, saying, "The militant blacks and women are most likely to break it [the convention] apart."

Yet each group was able to find some measure of satisfaction with the outcome. Caucus women could identify with the obvious success of the Women's and Black Caucuses; the non-caucus women supporting affirmative action saw the regulars and women coming together. Thus the dramaturgy of the Women's and Black Caucuses confronting the regulars with a non-negotiable demand that was partially accepted allowed both groups to see (a) women's goals achieved, and (b) their achievement a consequence of power wielded by groups with which they identified. For women opposing both the affirmative action proposals and the caucus groups, there remained the value of party unity.

Our theory predicts that those emerging satisfied with a conference outcome do so in part because they can attribute power (and thus some goal achievement) to a group with which they identify. The multiple group membership of most delegates were, then, resources for legitimation. In a sense, each delegate wanting unity could scan his identifications looking for those advantaged by the convention outcome. We would expect Women's Caucus members to increase their attribution of power to their own groups, and non-caucus women to see the power of regular groups enhanced by the proceedings.

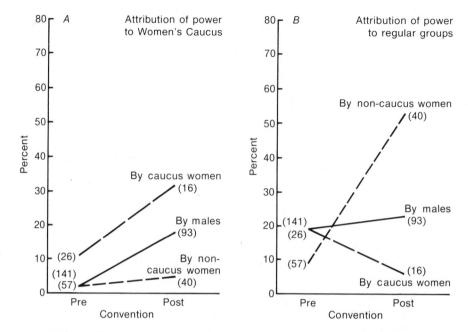

Figure 5.1
Caucus women see themselves as powerful and regulars as weak; non-caucus women see the Women's Caucus as weak and regulars as powerful.

A woman choosing a Women's Caucus role as her first or second most important role at the conference was considered a caucus woman. Power perception was measured by asking each delegate in the pre- and post-convention questionnaires which group would be (was) most powerful in determining the convention outcome. The following were considered "regular group" responses: Rules Committee, governor's conference at Hilton Head or at Kansas City, Democratic regulars, Charter Commission, DNC, Strauss, or state delegations. Statistical significance of change in power perception was measured by chi square, assuming pre and post samples to be independent. Power attribution changes were statistically significant at the .001 level for non-caucus women and males; for caucus women changes were not significant at the .05 level, possibly due to the small sample size (16).

The numbers enclosed in parentheses are the sizes of the samples on which the percentages are based.

Figure 5.1 displays the power attributions of women to the Women's Caucus and Democratic regulars in the pre- and post-conference period; the changes in power attributions are clearly in line with our theoretical expectations. In interpreting Figure 5.1 the reader should remember that the only fight of any consequence was over the affirmative action provision. Thus increases in power attributions to a group other than the Charter Commission must have been a consequence of the group's success in getting its way on the affirmative action provisions of the charter.

Note in Figure 5.1 how caucus and non-caucus women diverge in their power attributions to the Women's Caucus and regulars over the course of the convention. First, in Figure 5.1A the percentage of caucus women seeing their group as powerful increases from 11 to 32 percent, whereas by conference end only 5 percent of the non-caucus women see the caucus as powerful. Second, Figure 5.1B shows an even sharper divergence between caucus and non-caucus women in their perceptions of the power of regular groups; caucus women see regulars as less powerful by the end of the convention (a drop from 19 to 6 percent) while non-caucus women increase from 9 to 53 percent in their belief that party regulars were an important power center at the conference.

Male delegates, as Figure 5.1 shows, had what appears to be a more detached view of the Women's Caucus and party regulars; in both Figure 5.1A and 5.1B they are midway between caucus and non-caucus women in their power attributions. Yet, the percentage increase among males in attributing power to the Women's Caucus does support the caucus women's view of themselves more than it does the view of the non-caucus women (Figure 5.1A).

The interruption in regular proceedings forced by the Women's and Black Caucuses and the response of the Democratic leadership testified to caucus power—from which caucus members drew immense satisfaction. But from the perspective of regular Democratic women, the eventual affirmative action compromise was evidence of establishment power in forcing the caucuses to accept less than they had demanded.

Non-caucus women focused their attention on establishment efforts (the work of Strauss and the governors) and concluded that the regulars had shown their muscle. Members of the Women's Caucus claimed power for their own group because (a) the draft charter had been changed and (b) the interruption in regular proceedings had "stopped the show" and apparently caused a reconsideration by the leadership of the conference. Thus both Women's Caucus members and non-members ended up agreeing (a) that the affirmative action provision finding its way into the charter was acceptable and (b) that the Charter Conference had helped the party considerably.

In the end, then, women came to accept the charter and the conference by different paths—caucus women through affiliation with the caucus, and regular women through acceptance of the power of the party establishment.

Labor Delegates

For labor delegates, the problem of adjusting to the conference outcome—and thus their solution—was different. In fact, our data on labor delegates presented us with the following paradox. Labor caucus delegates (defined as those whose first or second choices described their Kansas City role as labor delegates) were, of all the groups we looked at, the most favorably disposed toward COPE. Only one labor delegate's score on our attitudinal measure on COPE was below the median for the entire sample. We next looked at the relationship between attitude toward COPE and (a) support for the affirmative action compromise and (b) ratings as to how helpful or harmful the Charter Conference had been. As we pointed out earlier, those liking COPE disliked the affirmation action compromise (Gamma $= -.43$) as well as being less enthusiastic on the helpfulness of the Charter Conference (Gamma $= -.30$). But to our surprise, labor delegates (by our pre-convention measure), who had been so supportive of COPE, did not share the views of COPE supporters toward the affirmative action compromise or the charter conference (see Table 5.1). In fact, of the non-caucus groups, labor delegates were among the stronger supporters of the affirmative action compromise and of the Charter Conference.

The apparent anomaly has a ready explanation. Over the course of the conference the leadership of COPE had articulated, and thus had come to symbolize, opposition to the affirmative action compromise and even to the conference as a whole. Thus a substantial portion of the variation in attitude toward COPE represented the impact of events during the convention. Yet the favorable attitude of labor delegates toward COPE had an obvious long-term basis formed over many years of activity on behalf of liberal union causes. Labor delegates did not suddenly change their attitude toward COPE; rather, they maintained a positive attitude but rejected COPE as a symbol of opposition to the affirmative action compromise and the conference in general. In the end the paradox was real; COPE spoke for non-labor delegates opposed to the charter and, as we shall see, other party groups spoke for the labor delegates.

Because the labor delegates were without effective leadership at the conference, we thought they might turn to more institutional sources of direction, responding to the same forces we earlier described in explaining the behavior of non-caucus women. That is, as labor came to see a failure in its leadership, it would find the power exercised by the Democratic regular groups reassuring. Thus we expected a sharp increase among labor delegates in attributions of power to Democratic regular groups. And if COPE had come to stand for opposition and dissatisfaction with what had taken place at Kansas City, we should expect an increase among COPErs in attributing power to disliked groups. As Figure 5.2 shows, the results bear out our expectations reasonably well. Both COPErs and labor delegates thought that labor groups would be powerful determinants of the conference outcomes. This hope suffered a severe reversal over the course of the convention; both COPErs and labor delegates agreed that the power of labor groups precipitously declined. But the two groups differed in ways that supported theoretical expectations concerning the power of party regular groups and caucus groups. For COPErs, the sharpest increase in power attribution occurred for the negatively valued caucus groups (see Figure 5.2A) and the smallest increase for party regular groups. At the conference's end, then, the most powerful groups in the eyes of the COPErs were the caucus groups and the weakest the labor groups. For labor delegates, the situation was the reverse. The sharpest increase in power attributions occurred for party regular groups and the smallest increase for caucus groups; at the convention's end, party regular groups were perceived as most powerful, followed by caucus groups and, lastly, by labor groups. Labor delegates adjusted their beliefs to reflect the increased power

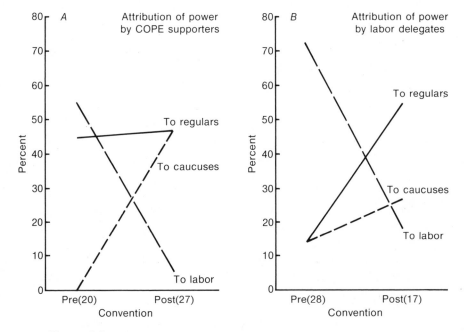

Figure 5.2
Labor delegates see themselves as weak and regulars as strong; COPErs see themselves as weak and caucuses as strong.

A COPE supporter was one who gave either a $+2$ or a $+3$ on the COPE attitude scale. A labor delegate was one who chose a labor role as either his first or his second most important role on the pre-conference questionnaire. For the measurement of power see the legend to Figure 5.1. For labor delegates, changes in power attribution were statistically significant by chi square at the .05 level; for COPErs at the .001 level.

of party regulars far more than COPErs did. Second, COPErs were far more negative toward the caucus groups perceived as gaining in power than were labor delegates. Thus for COPE, the adjustment of perceptions of power over the course of the conference must have confirmed their sense of loss. Labor delegates, on the other hand, accepted the loss of power but chose the more integrative device of attributing power to determine the outcome to well-liked groups seen as powerful.

The ways in which women and labor delegates came to terms with the affirmative action compromise show striking similarities. Those women feeling unrepresented by the leadership of the Women's Caucus found some measure of satisfaction in identification with Democratic regular leadership and its capacity to bring together conflicting groups. An anti-caucus forty-year-old Midwestern woman, whom we earlier quoted as wanting to "retreat from the exclusionary McGovern reforms" (what she thought of as a quota system), went on to say what a great job Strauss had done. On our post-convention questionnaire she added some special comments. She gave the affirmative action compromise of Saturday afternoon the highest possible praise as what she called "a peace-making gesture." But she added that its content was still somewhat disagreeable (-1 on our attitude scale).

A labor delegate from the Far West, dead set against what he called quotas, said, when asked what result he had wanted to see when he came to Kansas City,

> That's hard to say. . . . It's a big broad question. My answer there would be party unity—all the groups having a voice and to oppose any type of quota system.

Although he came to dislike the performance of Strauss he stayed supportive of the work of the Rules and Amendment Committee and the Charter Commission. Still, as he said, "I fear quotas two years from now." He accepted the affirmative action compromise as necessary for party unity.

Perhaps a more interesting case from our point of view is that of a middle-aged woman from the East Coast who saw her principal role as that of a labor delegate. She had supported Humphrey in 1972 and considered herself a strong Democrat. She was quite satisfied with the results of the Saturday compromise, saying,

> It was not quotas but the affirmative action that caused unity. I liked what happened but was surprised that there wasn't more debate and discussion from Southerners.

She strongly identified with Democratic establishment figures and their attempts to bring about compromise, while at the same time expressing a rather intense dislike of the Women's Caucus. Asked about the Women's Caucus, Terry Sanford, and Robert Strauss, she said,

> I resent women expecting things just because they're women. . . . Terry Sanford [of the Charter Commission] has done a fantastic job . . . and Robert Strauss . . . has done a good job.

The rather complete acceptance by women of the affirmative action compromise and the charter was due to representation of both reform and party establishment views among women and their ability to re-arrange perceptions of who "won" to fit their sentiments. Labor delegates, without effective leadership, adjusted by reaching out toward establishment groups, an adjustment helped by labor's close relationship with professionals.

Political Style: Purists and Professionals

We have cited a major proposition in the literature on political style that the party professional is more disposed than the purist to integrative solutions to political conflicts. From our theoretical perspective concerning legitimation, the professional's high concern for party unity is an incentive leading him to search for ways of interpreting political outcomes as advantageous to groups with which he is identified. At conventions most professionals are limited to audience roles, in which their principal work is psychological. Thus incentives like party unity lead delegates to rearrange what is in their heads rather than what is in the political world around them.

Second, professionals are far less likely than purists to put all their political eggs in one basket. Usually they come to conventions with a number of salient group identifications relevant to the proceedings. Success can be continually redefined so that a delegate always emerges as a winner as long as at least one group with which he is identified emerges triumphant. The purist, on the other hand, commits himself more fully to one group or policy goal. Success is defined as the achievement of that goal. The professional asks, "What goals can be achieved in this situation?" The purist asks, "Can I achieve my goal in this situation?" There is a world of difference between the two questions. The professional's concern for party unity leads him to search for the relatively advantaged groups with which he is identified. In the end he may be left with only party unity, but for the strong loyalist, it may be enough.

Kansas City tested the party professionals in three ways. First, they were faced with a substantive outcome tilted slightly toward the group caucus participants. Second, the professionals had to adjust to the caucus presence as a regular force in decision making. Finally, they had to control their obvious irritation at the Black Caucus' threat to bolt the convention unless its demands on affirmative action were met. Thus, when we correlated our index of party professionalism (the party professionals being those most strongly identified with party and preferring party unity to a correct charter, if it came to that) with support for the conference as a whole, we found a mildly negative correlation of $-.24$ (Table 5.1).

In our discussion of cleavages within the party in 1972 and 1974 (see Chaper 3), we drew attention to the conflict between purists and party professionals over the caucus movement. We pointed out that the most professionally oriented delegates disliked the caucuses (Gamma for Black Caucus $= -.47$, and for Women's Caucus $= -.45$), while the purists like them. Figure 5.3 shows changes in attributions of power among purists and professionals, as earlier figures did for labor and women. The model of political style, in conjunction with our notion of multiple group memberships, suggests that professionals, feeling some sense of loss, would be most prone to attribute power to establishment groups with which they are identified. Figure 5.3 shows changes in power attributions for purists and professionals from pre- to postconvention. An earlier analysis of group memberships of purists and professionals showed purists far more likely than professionals to identify with caucus groups and party professional more likely to ally themselves with traditional party groups—state and local constituencies, labor, and so on. At the convention, purists tended to identify with the liberal caucus Democratic Planning Group while the professionals affiliated themselves with the Coalition for a Democratic Majority. Thus purist groups in Figure 5.3 are DPG,

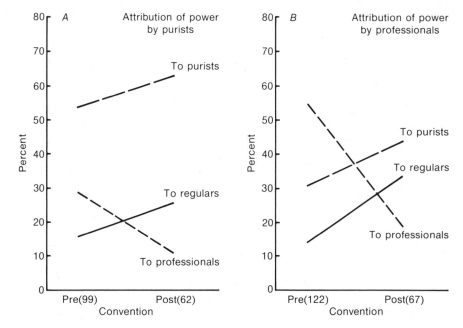

Figure 5.3
Purists see purist affiliate groups as powerful and others as relatively weak; professionals see professional affiliate groups as weak and both purist affiliate groups and regular groups as powerful.

A purist is one who values a correct charter over party unity; a professional is one who values party unity over a correct charter. Purist affiliate groups are DPG, Black Caucus, and Women's Caucus; professional affiliate groups are CDM and labor. Party regular groups are Rules Committee, DNC, Strauss, governors at Hilton Head or Kansas City, and state delegations. Power attribution changes were statistically significant for purists and professionals at the .001 level by chi square.

the Black and Women's Caucuses; the party professional groups are CDM and labor.

In the pre-convention period, as Figure 5.3 shows, both purists and professionals saw their own groups as powerful and other groups as weak. As our work on caucus institutionalization suggests, the power of purist groups was seen to grow by purists and professionals alike (the percentage growth being identical). Yet purists saw themselves as far more powerful than professionals (54 percent vs. 16 percent in Figure 5.3A) in the pre-convention period, and the difference persisted after the conference was over (63 percent vs. 26 percent).

For party professionals, as Figure 5.3B shows, the perceived decline in power of their own groups was combined with a perceived increase in power of purist groups. In the post-conference period, professionals saw purists and regular groups as quite close together. From the point of view of our theory, the change in power attributions to party regular groups—the party's Rules Committee, the Democratic National Committee, national chairman Strauss, the Democratic governors, and state delegations—is instructive. For professionals, the least integrative solution would have been to see a rise in the power of a strongly disliked group. But the dramaturgy of confrontation between caucus and establishment, combined with the ambiguity of the eventual compromise, allowed professionals to see power exercised both by the caucuses and by regular groups with whom professionals identified and felt comfortable. Thus there is a sharp rise in attributions of power to party regulars by party professionals. The purists, not feeling the necessity to explain losses in power, felt less compelled to change their attribution of power to regulars. Both purist and professional acknowledge the role of the party establishment in bringing about the compromise; the percentage of purists attributing power to the regulars rose from 16 percent in the pre- to 25 percent in the post-conference period, while the professionals increased from 14 percent to 34 percent. In the end, both purists and professionals saw party regulars as having played a powerful integrative role in bringing about a settlement. The dramaturgy of confrontation, with the Democratic establishment moving to occupy the center, produced both the appearance of success for purists and the avoidance of failure for professionals.

These results strongly support our theoretical notions concerning the role of purists and professionals in the process of legitimation. The professionals did seem to look for groups with which they were identified to which power flowed during the convention. Purists, on the other hand, were satisfied because they saw their own groups as being advantaged by the outcome.

Cleavage, Compromise, and the Preconditions
for Party Unity

To end the discussion of our theory of legitimation, it will prove useful to return for a moment to our earlier analysis of the evolution of political cleavage. The possibility of compromise is closely related to the nature of cleavage. In our earlier analysis, we pointed out the high loading of labor on the Democratic establishment or regular factor (see Figure 3.3, p. 56). The variety of establishment groups and persons—Strauss, DNC, Rules and Amendments Committee, state delegations, the Charter Commission, CDM—performed a most important integrative function. It made it particularly easy (1) for labor delegates to shift their support from COPE to other party establishment groups more advantaged by the outcome, and (2) for Democratic non-caucus women to accept the work of party establishment groups—Strauss, the governors, DNC, and so on—as legitimate. As long as the contending groups are clustered close together on a party-establishment dimension, it becomes correspondingly easier for party groups in the center to perform a brokerage function.

We can think of the dramatic confrontation at Kansas City as a battle between two groups, each representing a rather pure case of a party establishment group and a reform group. The potential membership of, say, the Women's Caucus was the pool of women delegates at the convention, of whom only 30 percent actually identified with the caucus. For these 30 percent it was vitally important that a settlement be worked out that advanced (a) what they thought of as women's issue goals and (b) women's organizational power goals. At the same time, if the settlement was not to cause a rift in women's ranks, non-caucus women would have to find some way to identify with another party to the negotiations—the Democratic regulars.

The solution, a change in wording of Article X, Section 6—but not the abolition of that section, as some in the Women's Caucus had initially demanded—enabled women who were strong on the establishment factor to support the result as well as women who were strong on the reform factor. With this solution there appeared to be complete solidarity among women, a result most wanted by the leadership of the Women's Caucus.

Thus far we have focused our attention on the multiple group memberships of the delegates as resources for legitimation. We have tried to show in some detail the mechanisms used by delegates to come to grips with their status as winners or losers. Such a system of legitimation works under rather special circumstances.

(1) The delegates to a convention can not be so committed to specific alternative provisions as to be immune to the arguments of group leaders. The reader may recall one of our basic propositions concerning the difficulties nominating conventions have with the legitimation process. The long pre-convention wind-up means that delegates come to the convention site with well-formed preferences in which they have made reasonably heavy psychological investments. Such commitments are not easy to change nor are they transferable from one candidate to another. If the majority of delegates had made similar investments during the Kansas City pre-convention period, leadership arguments might have fallen on deaf ears. Charter provisions, possibly by their nature, may discourage such investments.

(2) If there is no majority, or if a minority is sufficiently intense to use its capacity to disrupt as a bargaining point, then group leaders must have at their disposal a variety of alternative proposals for fashioning a compromise. A charter convention is a play on words, in which the alternatives are sentences fashioned on paper with pen or pencil (or mimeograph machines as was the case at Kansas City). In this way, charter conventions are different from modern nominating conventions. Dark horses emerging from smoke-filled rooms are, perhaps, historical analogues to the sentence on affirmative action (Article X, Section 6) that brought the contending groups together. But the idea of a compromise provision is still regarded as legitimate, whereas the dark-horse presidential candidate may have disappeared from the American scene. It is an issue to which we shall return in our discussion of the implications of our findings for the study of conventions and for the future of the nominating process.

Notes

1. Talcott Parsons and R. Bales, *Working Papers in The General Theory of Action* (New York: The Free Press, 1954). In the Parsons-Bales treatment there are four phases. We have taken certain liberties in reducing them to three.

2. V. O. Key, Jr., *Politics, Parties, and Pressure Groups* (5th ed; New York: Crowell, 1964), p. 431.

3. R. M. Koster, "Surprise Party," *Harper's Magazine*, March 1975, p. 30.

4. D. Broder, "Women, Minorities Look to '76," *Boston Globe*, December 9, 1974.

5. Ibid.

6. Ibid.

7. D. G. Sullivan et al., *The Politics of Representation* (New York: St. Martin's, 1974), p. 134.

6 Convention Decision Making: Some Theoretical Notes

In this chapter we shall trace some of the theoretical implications of our work on the evolution of cleavages, the institutionalization of arenas, and legitimation.

Cleavages

In *The Politics of Representation,* we discussed four dilemmas facing political parties. One of them concerned the balance between issue purity and organizational power. We phrased it as follows:

> Parties are organizations that must attract votes to survive. Yet, they also exist as instruments to achieve issues goals. Awareness of this dilemma on the part of a party's members creates a profound

organizational tension. Periodically, the tension comes to be expressed in the conflict between the professional politician and the issue purist, the latter willing to sacrifice power for integrity, and the former integrity for power. Over time, however, the tension seems to be resolved through the imperatives of organizational power driving out or transforming the issue purists. Thus the survival of issue concern may well depend on fresh infusions of personnel whose incentives for participation are directly related to important new issues.[1]

We pointed out in Chapter 3 that cleavages in 1968 on the substantive issues of war and race were coupled with challenges to the legitimacy of party decision-making processes. Amateur activists stormed the party citadel prepared to do battle with the tired professionals, mere buyers of votes in the eyes of the purists. The party regulars had been in power so long, so ran the charge, that they had misplaced their sense of issue integrity and were willing to resort to undemocratic practices to preserve their power in the party. Many of the regular Democrats felt as if they were being attacked by "crazies," by individuals with no conception of what politics required.[2] The organizational questions raised by the reformers, and countered by the regulars, were profound. They were again at issue in 1972, at Kansas City in 1974, and will be with us in 1976 and after. They challenge the classic model of convention decision making in the name of intra-party democracy.[3]

The myth of democratic participation—the notion that all the people should decide—exerts constant pressure on party organizations to expand the scope of participation in their affairs. Openness in delegate selection and intra-party democracy are so widely accepted as desirable that for their adherents they need no defense stronger than their utterance. The burden in argument is always on those who would limit the scope of participation and adopt less than democratic decision-making patterns.

The classic model of convention decision making is such a defense, for it advocates that party decision making be left in the hands of professionals. This means that there must be clear boundaries, difficult to cross, which separate the party professionals from the amateur activists who would seize the party in the name of their candidate and the issues he represents. If the barriers are sufficiently high, then the party and its convention delegations will be composed mostly of party activists, regardless of their issue or candidate commitments.

Thus the maintenance of barriers to entry into party councils means that the delegates who file into the convention hall on opening day will hold dear the notion that decisions should reflect the requirements of the party's organizational survival. The questions are not "Is he right on the issues?" Rather, organizational questions asked by the professionals are "Can he hold the party together should he get the nomination?" "Can he win?" "Can he govern if he wins so that four years hence the party will still be viable?"

The classic model, then, includes features restricting the scope of participation as well as a prescription for the patterns of decision making once the delegates are assembled. At Kansas City, the arguments of the reformers were not as simple. Few delegates had a comprehensive picture of party reform. Most were concerned principally with incremental changes in rules that would benefit themselves and the groups with which they were associated.

As we have shown in the preceding chapters, the affirmative action guidelines on delegate selection became the focal point for conflict at Kansas City. We suspect that the party professionals did not think of the affirmative action guidelines in either the draft or final charter as fostering openness. Rather, they saw the emergence of guidelines as an attempt by minority groups—blacks and women—to use their access to party decision making on the national level to force quotas on state and local units. Likewise, the advocates of increased social representation of minorities—blacks and women—saw themselves using the power of the national party to improve the representation of minorities in state and local parties.

Each group formed its view on the issue of centralization of party power and the affirmative action guidelines in terms of its own concrete interests. The abstractions of democratic theory were lost in the shuffle. The party professionals, who tended to define national party matters in terms of their positions in state and local parties, saw as their task minimizing the damage created by the charter conference. The advocates of increased social representation tended to think nationally because they had better access to power in national party affairs. Probably 90 percent of the delegates fell into one of the two categories. This gave the conference the air of a meeting of non-ideological, no-nonsense politicians.

Yet a minority at Kansas City saw an opportunity to bring the Democratic Party closer in organizational form to its vision of a "responsible" party. In Chapter 3 we called advocates of a "responsible" party the "centralizers." In their vision, in a democracy each party should offer the voters a coherent program; the party winning office should have sufficient power to carry out the program, and the voters should be able to hold the party responsible for its successes and failures in office. What is important in this model is that the party be a viable organization in which party membership is taken seriously and whose caucuses and conventions bind those who run for public office to support the party program.

In fact, in its original conception, the midterm conference was to consider "issues and policy," but chairman Robert Strauss and his supporters were able to focus the conference almost exclusively upon the party charter. The centralizing reformers desired a conference at which delegates from all levels of the party—Congress, national party structures, state level public and party officials, and citizens elected at the grass roots—would come together to debate and record their positions on the public policy choices facing the nation. They hoped that this would generate such support for those positions that public office holders at the national and state levels would be effectively, if not formally, bound to implement the choices made by delegates. The advocates of a more responsible party were serious. They proposed mandatory quadrennial policy conferences, a dues-paying party membership, and a variety of devices that would centralize power in the party. In their vision, a nationally centralized party would speak with one voice on the issues and thus transform American politics. This vision was not shared by the majority of delegates, who were more concerned with protecting or advancing a narrower interest.

What of the differences concerning organizational reform that had so animated the 1968 and 1972 conventions and promised to be divisive at Kansas City? First, did the cleavages persist in 1974? Second, was there still the impetus for sweeping reform that had characterized the reformers in 1968 and 1972? In our initial statement of the dilemma of issue purity vs. organizational power, we had hypothesized a gradual mending of the cleavage as the purists acceded to positions of power and responsibility in the party and as the professionals adjusted to new power centers in the party. As we pointed out in Chapter 3, our data do not show substantial changes in the cleavage structure between 1972 and 1974. Possibly two years is too short a time. Yet many of the original McCarthy supporters had been in local and state party leadership positions for some time. In 1974 the issue purity of the amateur activists who had supported McGovern in 1972 had not diminished substantially nor had the old McGovernites become more supportive of the party or its standard bearer, Hubert Humphrey.

But perceptions of power in the party had changed. All participants at Kansas City acknowledged the power of the major group caucuses, and their behavioral adjustments to the caucuses reflected that acknowledgment. Mayor Daley of Chicago said as much. In his speech to the delegates supporting the affirmative action compromise he said he knew power when he saw it and was prepared to make peace with the Black and Women's Caucuses. Professional politicians pride themselves on their understanding of power and its imperatives. Perhaps the growing institutionalization of the caucuses at Kansas City will promote a change in attitude toward the caucuses and their role in party decision making in 1976.

Summing up our conclusions on cleavages, three principal descriptive propositions stand out. (1) Because accommodation to shifts in power and organizational innovation (the role of caucuses) occurs so much sooner than changes in attitude toward the new power centers, the peace reached at Kansas City is very unstable. Innovation in organizations may generally be accepted on the cognitive level long before attitudes toward the innovation change. (2) The major cleavages at Kansas City over organizational issues, putting aside the centralizers, tended to reflect the narrower, more concrete interests of the major participants, not overarching ideological views of the role of the party. The party professionals acted to protect their power position in the party, and the group caucuses to advance theirs. (3) The cleavages first observed in 1968 and later in 1972 are still with the party; they will persist into 1976 and beyond.

Decision Making

The Democratic Party in the years 1968–1974 was a seedbed for experiments on delegate selection and decison making. Some of the experiments have brought new people into the party, others have created new organizational forms for making decisions. There are three basic questions one might pose concerning changes in decision making. (1) Will the decision-making patterns continue to involve bargaining between leaders of opposing hierarchical organizations? (2) If the answer to (1) is "yes," what will be the dominant hierarchical form—state and local party organization, candidate organization, or caucus group? (3) If the answer to (2) is some mixture of the three types of organization, how stable will the new organization be?

The Persistence of Hierarchical Organizations in Convention Decision Making

Democratic nominating conventions normally have around 3000 voting delegates. A town meeting format, in which any delegate can rise and speak his piece, is obviously out of the question. If a delegate wishes to make himself felt in the convention, he must join others so that his voice becomes loud and powerful enough to command the attention of others. Even if the delegate selection process could be arranged so that all delegates arrived at the convention process uncommitted, group formation would rapidly occur because it would give a powerful advantage to the groups committed most solidly to one candidate. Even if we prevented delegates from making formal commitments or pledges before the convention was convened, we would expect informal organization to flower in the pre-convention period, limited only by the cost of communication and transportation. Delegates would seek candidates, and candidates would ask for delegate commitments.

In politics the advantage goes to the strongest, and strongest means the group with the most votes. All of these considerations indicate that it is rational for a delegate to join a group. But there are psychological reasons as well for identification with and subordination to a group. Delegates have little time at the convention site to digest complex information, form a preference, and stick with it. Most delegates need groups with which they identify, that supply them with information, that keep them in the "know," and that give them a sense of being powerful at the convention.

State Delegation, Candidate Organization, or Group Caucus?

Our research at Miami and Kansas City presented us with the material for a fascinating experiment. The facts are these. In 1972, candidate organizations, state delegations, and group caucuses all seemed powerful and important the first day of the convention. Expectations were high. By the fourth day of the convention, the winning candidate organization was more powerful than others, the state delegations were viable, but the group caucuses had disintegrated. Interest in, attention to, and attendance at caucus meetings had fallen each day. The Youth Caucus was actually disbanded. In 1974 at Kansas City, the first day saw rather weak candidate organizations, strong state delegations, and strong caucus groups —especially blacks and women. Over the course of the convention, interest in and participation in the Black and Women's Caucuses increased. The major story of Kansas City was the success of the caucus movement. What can we conclude from the two stories?

Of course, the experiment we have described is not a perfect one. The composition of the delegations at the two conventions was different and the caucuses in 1974 had learned a thing or two since 1972. Yet the comparison is instructive. We think it allows formulation of the following rule: *When candidate organizations weaken, group caucuses increase in power and, of course, when candidate organizations increase in power, group caucuses weaken.*

How might this be explained? Let us return first to 1972. McGovern was successful because early in the campaign he presented himself as spokesman for those against the war, for blacks, and for women. Those groups were mobilized as McGovern supporters and some became delegates to the Miami convention, pledged to support McGovern. Commitment to McGovern was the calculated choice of many who saw his success in the nomination fight as the most effective way of realizing their goals. That choice, because it occurred early in the campaign, became a commitment hard to reverse. Thus many women, youth, and blacks were resistant to the arguments of the respective caucuses at Miami that the best way to achieve the goals of blacks, women, and youth was to respond to the leadership of these groups. For the most part, as McGovern moved toward the nomination, McGovern blacks, women, and youth moved away from identification with the caucuses.

Let us move now from Miami in 1972 to Kansas City in 1974. Candidate organizations were weak because (1) the charter would not become effective until 1980 and (2) the provisions under contention directly affected the narrow interests of party regulars, blacks, women, and other minorities. There was no need for a candidate focus. The delegates, freed from the cross-cutting allegiances we described in 1972, could give full attention to their caucus identifications. The salience of the group issues and the lack of candidate organizations facilitated the growth of caucus power.

Now let us go beyond the experiences of 1972 and 1974 and ask what would have happened in 1972 if the McGovern candidacy had failed. Remember that the typical McGovern supporter was reasonably weak in party loyalty and had been mobilized by specific issues to become a delegate. The failure of the McGovern candidacy would have released his supporters from their commitment. Where would they have gone? To another candidate organization or to group caucuses? In a multi-ballot convention, one might expect the group caucuses to become more important in mobilizing the purist supporters of defeated candidates. Blacks committed to McGovern and seeing him defeated would become more susceptible to caucus appeals. On the other hand, a regular

Democrat would tend to shift from the defeated candidate's organization to the one of the remaining viable candidate closest to his own issue position.

Thus the answer to our second question, concerning which organizational forms will dominate, is complex. In a single-ballot convention, candidate organizations will predominate. In a multi-ballot convention, there will be a mixture of candidate organizations, group caucuses, and state delegations.

Of course, these predictions are subject to modification as a consequence of changes in the political environment of conventions. A successful insurgent candidate will normally attract more than his share of purist delegate supporters. These delegates form most of the pool of potential caucus supporters simply because they are less strongly identified with party. In such years, the mix of candidate organizations, group caucuses, and state delegations should lean toward the more powerful caucus groups. In normal or non-insurgent periods, the reduced number of purist delegates will result in stronger candidate and state-delegation organizations.

Stability of Organizations and Their Goals at Conventions[4]

We began to answer our query concerning stability when we distinguished between single- and multiple-ballot conventions. Stated another way, the distinction is a way of talking about change over time. It was clear from our analysis that a major source of instability in organizational form concerns changes in goal orientation as a consequence of failure. The failure may stem from the inappropriateness of the goal for the occasion. Many delegates at Miami realized that the central purpose of the convention was to nominate a candidate, and thus quickly gave up any notion of achieving issue goals. In an analogous way delegates who came to Kansas City with the notion of promoting a particular candidacy soon realized their error and shifted to more immediate charter issue goals.

In general, then, goals not related to the central purpose of the convention are abandoned first. Thus *initial* instability in organizational forms is a consequence of shifts from task-irrelevant to task-relevant goals. At a nominating convention, purists coming to the convention with issue goals will contribute the most instability. Indeed, some of the early battles in Miami were instigated by McGovern leaders attempting to persuade caucus supporters to shift from an issue to a candidate goal. But in a multi-ballot convention, the sources of instability should begin to shift. We have predicted that in a multi-ballot convention the issue purists may well return to identification with and participation in caucus efforts. At this point the issue-oriented delegates would constitute an element of stability. From then on instability would be a consequence of regular delegates switching from one candidate organization to another. The organizational forms would remain reasonably stable, and the instability would revolve around which candidate organization was approaching a majority. Thus a multi-ballot convention will have an entirely different dynamic than a single-ballot convention.

Legitimation

Our research on Miami and Kansas City suggests that a convention is most likely to produce legitimation when (1) the candidate commitments of the delegates are psychologically revocable, (2) there is no issue polarization, (3) political styles are non-purist, (4) there is prospect of victory in the upcoming general election, (5) there are divisible prizes, (6) there are multiple group commitments, and (7) there is at least a minimal level of party loyalty.

We have argued at some length, both in Chapter 2 and Chapter 5, that developments in the postwar period have severely limited the applicability of the seven conditions to modern conventions, and thus reduced the prospects for legitimating conventions in the future.

The growth of national candidate organizations competing for delegates early in the pre-convention period means that a long period will have elapsed between the making of a commitment by a potential delegate and his arrival on the convention floor. Most delegates will have spent six or more months supporting the candidate to whom they have pledged themselves. That is a considerable psychological investment. If their candidate wins, all is well; if he loses, they may find it difficult to support an alternative candidate.

Not only do modern convention politics work to increase the intensity of commitment by delegates, but the kind of delegates recruited to conventions is changing. If one can generalize at all from the experience of the Democratic Party, non-incumbent presidential nominating conventions have opened up the delegate selection process considerably. This means a larger than normal number of issue purists surging into presidential politics to support a particular candidate. In general, the issue purists differ from others in terms of political style (condition 3 in our list), multiple group commitments (condition 6), and level of party loyalty (condition 7). The issue purist has not only invested time and energy in the support of one candidate; he does not have multiple goals that allow him to adapt to failure. If his candidate fails, he is likely to withdraw or become a member of a functional group caucus in an attempt to achieve his issue goals more directly. He is unlikely to shift his support to another candidate organization.

The multiple group commitments of party activists allow them to search for integrative solutions to failure. We documented this process in some detail as it occurred in Kansas City. The multiple group identifications of the delegates became the principal mechanism whereby the delegates preserved and enhanced their own sense of effectiveness. In other words, they acted in integrative ways that maintained their self-images as rational-instrumental political actors.

The party loyalty of these delegates provided an incentive for them to accept the outcome, to find an appropriate rationalization for continuing to support the party. Each delegate could use his multiple group memberships to discover a group to which he belonged that was relatively advantaged by the outcome; he could attribute power to that group. Bargaining between leaders at a convention is a drama arranged to provide most delegates at least one leading actor who represents them. The script must be carefully fashioned so that enough leading actors are perceived as powerful and effective bargainers to allow the multiple group memberships to come into play.

If such a system is to legitimate it requires the existence of an array of alternative candidates. As we pointed out at the end of Chapter 5, the success of Kansas City was due to the creation of the affirmative action compromise. A nominating convention, if it is to function in an analogous fashion, must have an array of real candidates representing different issue positions. These can no longer be dark-horse candidates. Modern notions of public decency require that parties do not spring new names on an unsuspecting public at convention time. Pre-convention campaigns must prepare the public for the possibility that any of eight or nine candidates might win.

This development implies a rather novel conclusion. If the revival of brokered conventions depends upon the existence of a number of candidates, then delegate selection rules that favor proportional representation may turn out to be especially desirable. They maximize the probability that a number of contenders will have established their credentials before the convening of the convention. From these may be chosen a compromise candidate who can attract the support of party rank-and-filers as well as the general public.

But whether a multi-ballot brokered or single-ballot convention, the seven conditions we described must be met—at least in part—if the convention process is to contribute to the legitimation of the party's nomination.

Notes

1. D. Sullivan et al., *The Politics of Representation* (New York: St. Martin's Press, 1974), pp. 2–3.
2. For views of purists and regulars, see A. Wildavsky, *Revolt Against the Masses* (New York: Free Press, 1972), p. 271.
3. Probably the best statement of the classic model is found in N. Polsby and A. Wildavsky, "Uncertainty and Decision Making at the National Conventions," in Polsby, Dentler, and Smith, *Politics and Social Life* (Boston: Houghton-Mifflin, 1963).
4. My formulation of the stability problem benefitted from discussions with Robert T. Nakamura of Dartmouth College.

CHAPTER 7

Nomination Reform and The Political System

The Classic Model and the Changed Political Environment

In the classic model of convention decision making, hierarchical party leaders bargain with each other to choose a nominee, and the various elements of the party come together at the end to support the winner. This model rests upon a number of assumptions about the political environment: that party leaders are able to exercise hierarchical authority; that they are able to remain uncommitted and thus retain a strong bargaining position vis-à-vis candidate organizations; and that potentially antagonistic elements in the party will agree to set aside their differences and work together for party victory.

But as we have seen, each of these assumptions has been thrown into doubt by changes in the American political system.

New delegate selection rules have limited the ability of state party leaders to exercise control over individual delegates. Changes in convention rules—including the abolition of the unit rule—have further weakened state delegation leaders.

Meanwhile, candidate organizations have been increasing in strength relative to party organizations. The growth in the number of state primaries has made it necessary for candidates to start building organizations early and to design appeals to larger audiences than just the party professionals. New campaign finance laws, by requiring candidates to raise money from numerous small donors in numerous states (in order to qualify for federal subsidies), have created another incentive to build large organizations early. Amateur activists, who provided the energy for the Goldwater, McCarthy, and McGovern campaigns, are eagerly sought by candidate organizations. These trends contribute to a further weakening of party organizations, and people who want to be delegates can easily understand the wisdom of identifying themselves with a candidate. It is no wonder that the percentage of delegates committed to a candidate before coming to the convention has increased sharply in recent years.

The final assumption of the classic model—that diverse elements of the party will agree to work together for victory in November—must also be questioned in light of recent experience. Both parties have undergone internal conflicts that were not healed at national conventions. At the Republican convention of 1964, a number of delegates opposed to Goldwater withheld support from the party's ticket, and a few even walked out of the convention. Democrats opposed to the Vietnam War staged a series of protests at their party's 1968 convention, and much effort in the ensuing campaign was spent in trying to bind up the wounds incurred at that meeting. At the 1972 Democratic convention, despite some rousing speeches for unification, opponents of McGovern's nomination had substantial reservations about the outcome.[1] The cleavage within the Democratic Party—based both on conflicting policy preferences and on conflicting styles—has been particularly severe. As we have seen in Chapter 3, it has persisted.

Thus, the capacity of party leaders to shape convention outcomes and the capacity of conventions to unify political parties cannot be taken for granted. These changes in party conventions reflect larger political trends: a decline in party identification[2]; an increase in issue voting, with its potential for polarizing the heterogeneous Democratic Party[3]; increased participation by amateur activists in presidential campaigns; and a growth in group-based activity by women and blacks, combined with the increased institutionalization of political efforts by those groups.

All of these developments pose serious problems for the classic model of convention decision making, and they pose problems for political parties as well. If conventions cannot provide, in V. O. Key's words, "a means for the contending candidates, factions, and interests within a party to consult and agree upon the terms on which they will work together,"[4] then their usefulness is severely limited. In the wake of recent presidential campaigns, it is no wonder that many observers have become concerned about the state of American parties' affairs and have suggested procedural changes to improve the situation. Let us examine some of the alternative paths for the future and the implications of following them.

Return to the Old Days?

Faced with the prospect of future non-unifying conventions and further arguments over the application of reform rules, some critics of the recent reforms have urged a return to pre-Reform Commission procedures.[5] Barriers to participation by amateur activists would be rebuilt, as state party committees would regain greater control over delegate selection. With party professionals once again in charge of conventions, the potential for controversy and for party splits would be reduced.

But it is far from clear that the Democrats would be able to return to the old ways of doing things. As the Kansas City conference demonstrated, blacks and women activists have substantially solidified their organizational positions since 1972, and their preferences are taken very seriously by party leaders. As the Kansas City experience also showed, these groups will strongly resist any attempt at what they feel is a move to dilute their strength at future conventions. The same is true of other people who have used the new reform measures to gain access to party affairs.

Even if it were politically feasible to abolish the reform rules, we must ask ourselves how desirable this change would be. The pre-reform era should not be romanticized. With regard to the 1968 convention, it should be remembered that there were a number of ways in which the nomination process had been closed to participation by those outside the inner circle of the state parties. As we have seen in Chapter 1, there were serious problems of timeliness, inadequate rules, and secrecy at various stages of the process. And we should not forget the marked underrepresentation of blacks, women, and young people at party conventions before 1972.

Party professionals are important forces for maintenance, stability, and integration within the organization. At Kansas City, high party officials were crucial in hammering out a final charter compromise. Their presence and visibility enabled delegates, even those who did not agree with the substance of the compromise, to feel that the result was at least legitimate.

But party professionals can also become devoted to the maintenance of their own organizational positions, and may move to insulate the organization from new constituency demands and political trends. As the late A. M. Bickel wrote in his insightful analysis of the nomination process,

> A party's professional cadre should, no doubt, have a voice. . . . Their greatest interest is the party's own institutional interest in winning—at least as it is vouchsafed to them to see that interest over the long run. But if they lend the party its character of an "organized appetite," as Felix Frankfurter once wrote, their appetite is sometimes keener for power in the organization than for organizing to secure the power of government. And in order to discharge the function that justifies the two-party monopoly of power, and that indeed makes it possible, the American major party must be a coalition formed every four years from a center of gravity that is apt to shift every so often. . . . Although each party has a professional cadre, and although each exerts its centripetal force from a different point on the spectrum of opinion and interest, each must also, therefore, be something of a new coalition every quadrennium. And each must open its nominating process sufficiently to enable itself to fulfill afresh its coalition-making function.[6]

Thus, limiting participation in the nominating process, besides creating problems for group representation and norms of procedural openness, may also constitute unwise electoral strategy.

It is tempting to yearn for a system in which an elite corps of moderate, pragmatic party professionals would meet together to keep conventions under control. But within the contemporary Democratic Party, it is difficult to identify a homogeneous professional elite that could hold such a meeting. There are splits along lines of issue and style within the Democratic National Committee, the various commissions created by that committee, and state party committees. As a result of recent nomination campaigns and party reforms, the membership of party bodies has changed. It is not at all clear that the "party elite" could itself hold a harmonious convention.

A National Primary

Given the hostility surrounding recent Democratic nominating procedures, and given the complexity of the party's rules for delegate selection, it is natural to search for ways to streamline and simplify the nominating process. (The complexity of the rules was painfully noticeable at Kansas City. Delegates, journalists, and—it must be admitted—political scientists all had difficulty comprehending the significance of changed commas and semicolons.) A recurring American response to this kind of complexity is to try to deal with it by turning the decision over to "the people." Why not substitute a direct national primary for the present blend of state primaries, state conventions, and national convention?

There are a number of problems with a national primary. First, some difficult procedural questions must be answered. Would a majority be necessary for nomination, or only a plurality? (If a plurality rule prevailed a party might find itself with a nominee who was the choice of only a minority faction.) Would there be a provision for a runoff in the event that no candidate achieved a specified percentage of the vote? What would be the criteria for deciding how many candidates could participate in a runoff? If a goal of a national primary is to shorten and simplify the nomination process, then a series of runoff elections begins to look less than ideal.

The institution of a national primary would raise particularly serious problems for candidates who lacked the necessary resources to mount campaigns simultaneously in all fifty states. In the present system, candidates (like Eugene McCarthy in 1968 and George McGovern in 1972) who start with relatively few resources can parlay early primary victories into increased support as the nomination process goes on.

Another problem with national primaries is that *all* the crucial decisions would be made by rank-and-file voters—or, more accurately, those voters who were registered and who bothered to turn out. (Turnout for presidential primaries has not been high in the past.) The combined state-primaries/state-conventions/national-convention system provides multiple tests for a candidate and potential President. He must be able to appeal both to rank-and-file voters and to the party activists who become delegates to a national convention. But with a national primary, the special role of delegates would disappear. It could be argued that this would reduce the quality of decision making, since research has shown that delegates are better informed than the rank-and-file about both issues and candidates.[7] Defenders of the convention system argue that those who vote in primary elections (given the absence of party labels as a guide) are likely to base their decisions on name familiarity, ethnic background, and other criteria not necessarily related to the selection of a good President.[8] In contrast, convention delegates may well have had contact with the candidates and are often familiar with their records and views.

Finally, the introduction of a national primary would further the trend toward the atrophy of political parties. The chance to go to a nominating convention is a prize to which party workers can aspire; thus the hope of convention attendance has often been an incentive for party workers to perform necessary volunteer tasks. Although the new rules limit the ability of state party committees to select delegates to national conventions, a number of such appointments can still be made. Besides offering incentives for participation in party affairs, a national convention also provides an opportunity for party members to get together and hammer out a common platform. This process worked surprisingly smoothly for the Democrats in 1972.[9] (Even if a national primary were adopted, there could be a special platform convention. But it is doubtful that a process of platform writing divorced from that of presidential selection would be taken nearly as seriously.) The bypassing of national conventions would constitute yet another—perhaps fatal—blow to our beleaguered party system.

The Present System

Another possible choice for the future, of course, is to keep the present system—perhaps with some incremental changes in response to particular demands of a changing political environment. Under the post-1968 reforms, the Democratic Party's nominating process has been made considerably more open. Delegates now must be chosen in the year of the convention itself. Further, in accordance with national party guidelines, state parties have under-taken to publicize delegate selection meetings and to open these meetings to broader participation by interested Democrats.

Groups who had been underrepresented—blacks, women, and young people—took advantage of affirmative action rules to increase their participation at the 1972 Democratic convention. As we have seen earlier in the study, the percentages of blacks and youth at the 1974 midterm conference were somewhat lower than they had been in 1972, while the percentage of women in 1974 remained at the 1972 level. The experience of Kansas City suggests that the institutionalized Black and Women's Caucuses will be strong forces pressing for their groups' representation at future nominating conventions. Organized youth groups, who met sporadically at the 1972 convention and who were not in evidence at Kansas City, can be expected to be less of a force.

Although the gains in openness and group representation are clear, some critics have maintained that the new reform rules created a convention in 1972 that was dominated by uncompromising, ideological amateurs.[10] We have shown elsewhere, however, that empirical evidence does not support that view.[11] McGovern delegates were willing to compromise in the interests of their candidate, and decision-making patterns at the 1972 convention were similar to those at previous party meetings.

Still, there is no question that, given present circumstances, the Democratic Party's nomination process is filled with potential dangers. Neither the 1968 nor the 1972 convention had the legitimating and unifying effects that political scientists have celebrated. And Chapter 3 of this book provides evidence of a continuation of the cleavages that have plagued the party in its recent past. (The Republican Party, of course, is not immune to cleavages. The 1964 convention and internal party conflicts in the 1976 campaign offer ample proof of divisions within that party.)

It might be argued that the present system, by opening the nomination process to wider participation and by creating guidelines for group-based representation, makes it impossible for effective bargaining—and ultimately unifying—to take place. But it seems to us that the conditions that facilitate or frustrate a legitimating convention go beyond a particular set of delegate selection rules. The preconditions for legitimation may be stated as follows: First, the issues dividing factions of the party cannot be of such magnitude that they make each potential compromise seem a betrayal of the vital interests of any major faction. Second, the style differences (professional vs. amateur) between factions cannot be so marked that they engender distrust and hostility (as was the case in 1968 and 1972).[12] Finally, there must be a reasonably good chance to win the Presidency; when the prospects for winning the general election are poor, the incentive for party unity weakens.[13] (One of the factors promoting unity at the Kansas City conference was the feeling among delegates that, given the deteriorating economic situation and the party's substantial congressional gains the month before, the Democrats would have a good chance to regain the White House in 1976.)

If these preconditions of legitimation are not met, no set of delegate selection and convention rules can magically create them. And if the present system of rules does not result in party unity, the reasons for that outcome go beyond the rules themselves. Still, is there anything that could be done to increase the probability that a convention will result in unity and legitimation?

The Search for a Legitimating Convention

Given the contemporary political environment, the continued existence of nominating conventions, and a relatively open delegate selection process, what could be done to increase the orientation of delegates toward legitimation? Of course, the problem would be made much smaller by the emergence of an issue on which a party's factions agreed and that improved the party's prospects for victory. Continued economic difficulty, which helped to forge unity in Kansas City, could increase the orientation toward legitimation at future Democratic meetings. Another way out of the problem would be to find a strong presidential candidate acceptable to all factions. (The attractiveness of this solution explains party members' enthusiasm for a Ted Kennedy candidacy in 1976, even in the face of the senator's repeated denials of interest in the nomination.)

Barring such *deus ex machina* solutions, are there other ways by which legitimation prospects at nominating conventions could be increased? Perhaps the experience of the 1974 Charter Conference can provide some clues. As we have shown in Chapter 5, an impressive degree of legitimation did take place at Kansas City—but a charter conference has certain characteristics that facilitate compromise and party unity. First, instead of one big prize (the presidential nomination), there are a number of smaller prizes (the charter provisions). It is thus possible for a delegate to lose on one provision and win on another. Second, the ambiguity of each provision and the uncertainty as to its consequences allows delegates to interpret the adoption of the provision as being in their own interest. Finally, compromise can be achieved rather easily—by adding a few words or changing the punctuation.

At a nominating convention, by contrast, there *is* one big prize—the presidential nomination. This makes it much harder for losers to interpret defeat as victory. But there are other, smaller prizes at a nominating convention—the platform and the vice-presidential nomination, for example. By their restrained behavior on the 1972 platform committee, McGovern delegates were able to preserve a spirit of good will within that committee.[14] The platform offers a good opportunity for the dominant faction to show generosity, for (unlike the case of credentials) yielding ground on the platform does not hurt its candidate's chances for the nomination. The tradition of a "balanced ticket" shows that presidential nominees have also used the prize of the vice-presidential nomination to mollify the losing faction. Although some reformers, in the name of democracy, have urged that the vice-presidential choice be thrown open to the convention delegates, we believe that the presidential candidate would be much more likely than rank-and-file delegates to choose a member of a different faction and thus enhance the prospects of unity.

Besides the existence of multiple prizes, other resources for legitimation at Kansas City were provided by the multiple group memberships of many delegates. Ties to multiple groups made it possible, even for delegates who were not happy with the substance of the compromise, to identify with a group that seemed to be doing well at the conference. Thus, women who did not identify with the Women's Caucus were able to take pride in the conference performance of regular party leaders. Knowing that multiple group memberships aid legitimation does not lead to any clear policy recommendation. But it does suggest that if the amateur activists of 1968 and 1972 continue to attain positions in regular party organizations, they will experience loyalties to more than one group within the party and will become more oriented toward party unity. Thus, it might aid eventual unity if party organizations at all levels would open their activities to wider participation in other areas than delegate selection.

Going beyond activities at the convention itself, it would be in the interests of legitimation to adopt before the convention a strong set of agreed-upon procedures for resolving delegate selection disputes. This, of course, is easier said than done. Some would argue that the multiple reform rules, party commissions, and compliance review bodies will be the focal points for new and bigger conflicts among party factions. But to the extent that the members of the party's review bodies are widely respected (and candidate-neutral) party figures, perhaps some of the factional wrangling could be dissipated in the months before the convention.

Delegate Selection, Party Conventions, and the Political System

Unfortunately for those who would like to solve a party's problems by writing a new set of rules, convention behavior is closely linked to forces in the political system as a whole. Rule changes can alter the distribution of power within a party, but they cannot abolish the realities of underlying political trends. No set of rules can make the issue and style polarization in the Democratic Party disappear, or arrest the decline in party identification, or erase the tension between special group caucuses and traditional party organizations.

Although political scientists have looked to flexible, pragmatic party professionals to facilitate and mediate the bargaining between factions, it is sometimes hard to find these flexible people in the midst of a heated conflict over a presidential nomination. In 1972, even the supporters of regular candidates began to show marked purist tendencies after they lost the nomination.[15] It is, not surprisingly, hard to be a good loser. But unless a strong group of people is present who can talk to multiple factions and help to forge party unity, then the prospects for legitimation are dim indeed. With current pressures to announce candidacies and commit support early, the incentives for people to remain neutral are few. But if a convention contains a group that has both prestige and credibility with diverse factions, then hostility can be moderated. The Democratic governors, liberal labor leaders, and national party officials played this role at Kansas City, working both privately and publicly for compromise. Whether such professional behavior will occur often under the pressures of a presidential nomination battle is an open question.

Although we should have liked to offer the hope and certainty that a set of crucial procedural changes could usher in an age of legitimating conventions, we concede our inability to do so, for conventions cannot seal themselves off from the rest of the political world.

Notes

1. See Sullivan et al., *The Politics of Representation* (New York: St. Martin's, 1974), Chapter 5.

2. See W. D. Burnham, "American Politics in the 1970's: Beyond Party?" in W. N. Chambers and W. D. Burnham, eds., *The American Party Systems* (2nd ed.; New York: Oxford University Press, 1974).

3. A. H. Miller, W. E. Miller, A. S. Raine, and T. A. Brown, "A Majority Party in Disarray: Policy Polarization in the 1972 Election." Paper delivered at the 1973 annual meeting of the American Political Science Association, New Orleans.

4. V. O. Key, Jr., *Politics, Parties, and Pressure Groups* (5th ed.; New York: Crowell, 1964), p. 431.

5. See, for example, Coalition for a Democratic Majority, *Towards Fairness and Unity for '76* (Washington: CDM, 1973).

6. A. M. Bickel, *Reform and Continuity* (New York: Harper, 1971), pp. 41–42.

7. See H. McClosky, "Are Political Conventions Undemocratic?" *The New York Times Magazine*, August 4, 1968. Also see H. McClosky, P. J. Hoffman, and R. O'Hara, "Issue Conflict and Consensus among Party Leaders and Followers," *American Political Science Review*, 54 (June 1960), pp. 406–427.

8. For a good discussion of the implications of a national primary, see N. W. Polsby and A. B. Wildavsky, *Presidential Elections* (3rd ed.; New York: Scribner's, 1971), pp. 234–253.

9. See Sullivan et al., *The Politics of Representation*, Chapter 4.

10. See, for example, J. A. Center, "1972 Democratic Convention Reforms and Party Democracy," *Political Science Quarterly*, 89 (June 1974), pp. 325–349; and Coalition for a Democratic Majority, *Towards Fairness and Unity for '76* (Washington: CDM, 1973).

11. Pressman and Sullivan, "Convention Reform and Conventional Wisdom," *Political Science Quarterly*, 89 (Fall 1974), pp. 539–560.

12. For a perceptive account of friction over style differences in 1968, see Wildavsky, "The Meaning of 'Youth' in the Struggle for Control of the Democratic Party," *The Revolt against the Masses* (New York: Basic Books, 1971), pp. 270–287.

13. For an expanded discussion of the preconditions of legitimation, see Sullivan et al., *The Politics of Representation*, pp. 127–132.

14. Ibid., Chapter 4.

15. Ibid., Chapter 5.

Pre-conference Questionnaire, Mailed November 12, 1974

1. Were you a voting delegate at any of these Democratic presidential conventions? (Circle appropriate years)

   1960   1964   1968   1972   Others _____

2. Most recent party office held _____

   Dates _____

3. Most recent elective office held _____

   Dates _____

4. Who is closest to being your ideal candidate for the Democratic presidential nomination in 1976? _____

5. Do you think he or she will make a serious attempt to win the nomination? _____

6. If he or she does not run, which of the active candidates do you prefer?

   _____

7. Are you actively supporting a presidential candidate? _____

8. Just prior to the 1972 convention, who was your first choice for a presidential candidate? _____

9. Circle the name of the candidate whose chances for the presidential nomination in 1976 will be most affected by the outcome of the conference.

   Wallace   Jackson   Mondale   Bentsen   Other _____

10. As you think about your participation in the Kansas City conference, which of the following *best* identifies you? *Next best?* (Put "1" for best, "2" for next best)

Liberal ____	Conservative ____	Wallace supporter ____	Jackson supporter ____
Democratic Planning Group ____	Coalition for a Democratic Majority ____	Black Caucus ____	labor union ____
Women's Caucus ____	McGovern supporter ____	Youth caucus ____	Mondale supporter ____

11. Generally speaking, do you think of yourself as (*Circle one*)

    Strong   Not strong   Independent   Other _____
    Democrat   Democrat

12. What is your most important concern at this conference? (Use "1" for most important . . . "2" . . . "3" . . . "4" for least important.)

    _____ To create a correct charter
    _____ Helping your preferred candidate for 1976
    _____ Keeping the Democratic Party together
    _____ Achieving the goals of your group within the party

13. Which of the following charter issue votes are you most concerned about? (*Circle one*)

    Affirmative   Proportional   Judicial   Other _____
    action   representation   Council   _____

14. If you *had* to choose, which is most important? (*Circle one*)

    Writing a correct charter   Making sure the party stays together

15. Where do you expect the most important decisions at the conference to be made? (*Circle one*)

    State delegations
    Special caucuses (e.g., Black, Women, labor, etc.)
    Coalition groups, such as the Coalition for a Democratic Majority, the Democratic Planning Group, etc.
    Presidential candidate organizations
    On the conference floor
    Was or will be decided before the convention

16. Which of these groups do you think will be most powerful in determining the nature of the charter? (*Circle one*)

Democratic Planning Group	Coalition for a Democratic Majority	Black Caucus
Labor caucus	Women's Caucus	Youth caucus
Wallace organization	Mondale organization	Jackson organization

Other _____

17. Racial/ethnic group: (*Circle one*)

Black   Chicano   Asian   White   Native American

Other _____

18. Sex: Male   Female

19. Age: 18–24   25–35   36–50   51–65   65+

20. Education:

| Less than high-school graduate | High-school graduate | Some college | College degree |
| Some graduate or professional | Professional degree (field) _____ | | |

Interview Form
Used at Conference Site,
December 6–8, 1974

Delegate Interview

DELEGATE NAME: _____

INTERVIEWER NAME: _____

DAY OF INTERVIEW: FRI   SAT   SUN

TIME OF INTERVIEW: _____ AM   PM

PLACE OF INTERVIEW: _____

1. How are you enjoying the conference thus far? (PROBE FOR DIF-
FICULTIES IN ORIENTING TO CONFERENCE TASKS)

Do you think that midterm conferences should be held in the future?
(PROBE PRO OR CON ANSWERS: Why? Why not? What are the
benefits? What are the costs? Etc.)

3. When you came to Kansas City, what results did you most want to see come out of the conference? (WRITE IN DELEGATE'S WORDS BELOW; THEN CODE RESPONSE BELOW, USE A "1" FOR *MOST IMPORTANT*)

INTERVIEWER CODING	PROBES
____ TO CREATE A CORRECT CHARTER	What should that charter look like? What provisions? What should it do?
____ HELPING PREFERRED CANDIDATE FOR 1976	Who? Will this hurt or help your candidate? Are you campaigning now?
____ KEEPING THE PARTY TOGETHER	Is this happening? What is necessary for this to occur? Who would be at fault if rupture occurred?
____ ACHIEVING THE GOALS OF DELEGATE'S GROUP	What goals? How accomplished? What costs are you willing to bear for goal?
____ SPECIFIC PLANK IN CHARTER	Which planks? What positions? Why?
____ OTHER: _____	

FIRST IF TWO REPLIES: Which of these is more important? (CODE 1 & 2)

IF ONE REPLY: Anything else? (CODE RESPONSE AS "2")

THEN PROBE ANSWER USING PROBES ABOVE! WRITE ANSWER IN BELOW

4. Do you still feel the same way? (I.E., THAT "1" ABOVE IS MOST IMPORTANT)

1. YES   2. NO   3. UNDECIDED

IF YES, GO TO QUESTION 6
IF NO OR UNDECIDED, ASK QUESTIONS 5A and 5B

5A. Well, as of right now, what results do you want most? (WRITE DELEGATE'S WORDS BELOW; THEN CODE RESPONSE)

____ TO CREATE A CORRECT CHARTER	What should that charter look like? What provisions? What should it do?
____ HELPING PREFERRED CANDIDATE FOR 1976	Who? Will this hurt or help him? Are you now campaigning for him?

_____ KEEPING THE PARTY
TOGETHER

Is this happening? What is necessary for this to occur? Who would be at fault if rupture occurred?

_____ ACHIEVING GOALS OF
DELEGATE'S GROUP

What goals? How accomplished? What costs are you willing to bear for that goal?

_____ SPECIFIC PLANK IN
CHARTER

Which planks? What positions? Why?

_____ OTHER _____

FIRST IF TWO REPLIES: Which of these is more important? (CODE 1 & 2)

IF ONE REPLY: Anything else? (CODE AS 2)

THEN PROBE ANSWER USING PROBES ABOVE, WRITE ANSWER IN BELOW

5B. What changed your mind?

6. What do you find is the best way of keeping in touch with conference developments? Which groups or individuals have been most helpful to you in this regard?

7. Now we would like you to indicate your attitudes toward the following groups on a scale of +3 to −3 (plus three to minus three). On this scale, how would rate the DNC? What about the Women's Caucus? Etc.

GROUP	RATING	COMMENTS IF ANY
DNC	_____	_____
WOMEN'S CAUCUS	_____	_____
BLACK CAUCUS	_____	_____
LABOR CAUCUS	_____	_____
STATE DELEGATION	_____	_____
DEMOCRATIC PLANNING GROUP	_____	_____
COALITION FOR A DEM. MAJORITY	_____	_____
THE DEMOCRATIC PARTY	_____	_____
RULES AND AMENDMENTS COMMITTEE	_____	_____

Now could you do the same for some individuals?

TERRY SANFORD   _____   _____

GEORGE WALLACE   _____   _____

MORRIS UDALL   _____   _____

HENRY JACKSON   _____   _____

LLOYD BENTSEN   _____   _____

ROBERT STRAUSS   _____   _____

GEORGE McGOVERN   _____   _____

HUBERT HUMPHREY   _____   _____

TED KENNEDY   _____   _____

BIRCH BAYH   _____   _____

8. How do you think what happens (has happened) here will affect the future of the Democratic Party?

Thumbnail Sketch of Delegate

SEX: FEMALE   MALE

AGE: 18–25   26–30   31–40   41–50   51–60   61–70   70+

RACE: ASIAN   BLACK   CHICANO
         NATIVE AMERICAN   WHITE

DESCRIBE ANY OUTSTANDING PHYSICAL CHARACTERISTICS (DRESS, TIDINESS, CAMPAIGN BUTTONS, CAUCUS BADGE, ETC.)

DESCRIBE DELEGATE'S ATTITUDES TOWARD CONFERENCE AS A WHOLE (IF OBSERVED) (ELATED AND ENTHUSIASTIC, CASUAL, DISTURBED, DISCOURAGED, ETC.)

DESCRIBE DISCERNIBLE ATTITUDE TOWARD BEING INTER-VIEWED (RELUCTANT, HURRIED, FRIENDLY, COOPERATIVE, ETC.)

JOT DOWN ANY OTHER MISCELLANEOUS INFORMATION HELPFUL TO UNDERSTANDING DELEGATE'S RELATIONSHIP TO CAUCUS GROUP, CONFERENCE, DELEGATION, ETC.)

Post-conference Questionnaire

APPENDIX III

1. What turned out to be your most important concern at the Kansas City conference? (Use "1" for most important ... "2" ... "3" ... "4" for least important)

   _____ To create a correct charter
   _____ Helping your preferred candidate for 1976
   _____ Keeping the Democratic Party together
   _____ Achieving the goals of your group within the party
   _____ Other _____

2. Using a +3 to −3 rating scale (+3 for most favorable and −3 for most unfavorable), indicate your attitude toward:

   The Charter Commission provisions adopted by the conference on:
   _____ Proportional   _____ Affirmative   _____ Judicial
         representation   action   Council
   _____ The eventual compromise as adopted by the conference on affirmative action.
   _____ COPE (headed by Al Barkan)   _____ Labor as a whole
   _____ Black Caucus at   _____ Women's Caucus   _____ Latino caucus
         the conference   at the conference   at conference

3. Using a +3 to −3 rating scale (+3 for Helped a Lot and −3 for Hurt a Lot), how much do you think the Kansas City conference either helped or hurt the Democratic Party? _____

4. Generally speaking, do you think of yourself as: (*Circle one*)

Strong   Not strong   Independent   Other _____
Democrat   Democrat

5. How will the new party charter affect the political power of the following? (Use "+" for enhance, "0" for no change, "−" for decrease)

____ Presidential   ____ DNC   ____ State   ____ Democratic
     candidate   parties   congressional
     organizations   caucus

____ Rank &   ____ National
     filers   chairperson

6. Where do you think the most important decision concerning the conference was made? (*Check one*)

____ Before the conference in such places as the Governors' Conference in South Carolina, DNC Hdqtrs. in Washington, etc.
____ Special caucuses (e.g., Black, Women, Latino, labor, etc.)
____ Coalition groups such as Democratic Planning Group, The Coalition for a Democratic Majority
____ Presidential candidate organizations
____ State delegations
____ Behind the podium in small groups of leaders
____ Rules and Amendments Committee
____ On the floor
____ Other _____

7. Which group listed below was most powerful in determining the nature of the charter? (*Circle one*)

Democratic Planning   Coalition for a   Black Caucus
Group   Democratic Majority

Labor caucus   Women's Caucus   Latino caucus

Jackson   State
organization   delegations (List) _____

Other _____

8. As you think about your participation in the recent Kansas City conference, which of the following *best* identified you? *Next best?* (Put "1" for best, "2" for next best)

Liberal ____   Conservative ____   Wallace   Jackson
                                        supporter ____   supporter ____

Democratic   Coalition for   Black   Labor
Planning   a Democratic   Caucus ____   union ____
Group ____   Majority ____

Women's   McGovern   Latino   Other ____
Caucus ____   supporter ____   caucus ____   _____

9. Who is closest to being your ideal candidate for the Democratic presidential nomination in 1976? _____

10. Do you think he or she will make a serious attempt to win the nomination? _____

11. If he or she does not run, which of the active candidates do you prefer?

    _____

12. Which of the potential candidates for the presidential nomination did you make an effort to see, hear, or obtain information about? _____

    _____

Index